May, 1999

For Bob + Cynthia —

May all you

tastes of Japan

be fabulous —

Love,

Ellen

A TASTE OF JAPAN

A TASTE

food fact
and fable

customs and
etiquette

OF JAPAN

what the
people eat

Donald Richie

KODANSHA INTERNATIONAL
Tokyo • New York • London

for Ona

The text of this book is based on a series of articles that appeared in *Winds* magazine, 1981-83.

Excerpt adapted from *Empire of Signs* by Roland Barthes, translated by Richard Howard. Translation copyright © 1982 by Farrar, Straus and Giroux, Inc. Reprinted by permission of Hill and Wang, a division of Farrar, Straus and Giroux, Inc.

Distributed in the United States by Kodansha America, Inc., 114 Fifth Avenue, New York, N.Y. 10011, and in the United Kingdom and continental Europe by Kodansha Europe Ltd., 95 Aldwych, London WC2B 4JF. Published by Kodansha International Ltd., 17-14 Otowa 1-chome, Bunkyo-ku, Tokyo 112, and Kodansha America, Inc. Copyright © 1985 by Kodansha International Ltd. All rights reserved. Printed in Japan.
First edition, 1985
First paperback edition, 1992
96 97 98 99 10 9 8 7 6 5 4

LCC 84-48696
ISBN 4-7700-1707-3

In this book, all twentieth-century Japanese names appear in Western order, and all earlier names appear in traditional order, surname first.

CONTENTS

PREFACE

Most people now like Japanese food. Yet those many eating *sashimi* and *rāmen* alike still know very little about it. They do not know the context of the cuisine: how the food fits into Japanese life, what its history has contributed, how it is properly chosen and consumed, what it all *means*.

A cuisine is a cultural expression and without some understanding, both culture and cuisine are unappreciated. This book attempts an explanation. It is about ordinary Japanese cuisine, its history, its place in Japanese life. It describes the dishes but not the processes. It tells how to eat the food but not how to prepare it. It attempts to allow the reader to view Japanese food as the Japanese themselves do.

The cooking covered in this book is not the special cuisine sometimes given foreigners, but the ordinary and everyday dishes of the Japanese themselves. For this reason such specialized cuisines as *kaiseki* (tea ceremony food) and *shōjin ryōri* (temple food) are not included. It is the rare foreigner who partakes of such, and it is the rarer Japanese.

In writing these chapters I am indebted to many different sources of information, far too many for me to mention them all. I would, however, like to acknowledge the help given me by Michiyo Kashiwagi. She caught errors, offered new facts, and made helpful suggestions. Thanks to her, my book became a better one.

INTRODUCTION

The dinner tray seems a picture of the most delicate order: it is a frame contain-ing, against a dark background, various objects (bowls, boxes, saucers, chopsticks, tiny piles of food, a little gray ginger, a few shreds of orange vegetable, a background of brown sauce), and since these containers and these bits of food are slight in quantity but numerous, it might be said that these trays fulfill the definition of painting. . . . However, such an order, delicious when it appears, is destined to be undone, recomposed according to the very rhythm of eating . . . the painting was actually a palette.

—Roland Barthes

The cuisine of Japan is in many ways different from those of other countries. Dif-ferent kinds of food, different ways of cooking, of serving—different ways too of thinking about food, eating, meals.

Where to begin among all the differences? Well, most cuisines emphasize the large—big portions, healthy helpings; only in Japan, and in Japanese-inspired styles such as *la nouvelle cuisine*, is the small considered satisfying. Small but lots, however; a traditional meal is made up of a variety of little portions. Not then the mighty American steak, the French stew, or the Chinese fish, but something much smaller.

And something usually already cut up or in some way made instantly edible as, say, the sizzling steak is not. In the West, indeed, a part of culinary pleasure comes from the ritual dismembering of the roast or the standing crown of ribs. In China as well, the moment of the crumbling of the charcoal-broiled carp, the opening of the clay-baked fowl, are part of the gustatory experience.

Not so in Japan. Here the portions arrive already cut up into bite-sized pieces or are small enough to be easily broken at the table. One of the reasons given for this is that the Japanese use chopsticks, instruments not ideal for cutting and slic-ing. But then, so do the Chinese and many another Asian country as well, and these cuisines do not insist on small portions being cut into bite-sized pieces before being served.

The reason is not chopsticks. It is, I think, a great concern for the presentation of the food, its appearance. To be sure, food everywhere must be presentable. Things must look, in the Western phrase, "good enough to eat." But there the matter usually ends. Not, however, in Japan. It is enough, in America and Europe, that a steak look like a steak, a chicken like a chicken. In Japan, while fish should look like fish, the fish dish ought also to look like something more. It ought to reflect within its composition another concern, one the West considers aesthetic. The effect should be as pleasing to the eye as the taste is to the tongue. At the same time, there is a canon of presentation, a system of culinary aesthetics to be satisfied.

This, then, is one of the reasons for small portions and plate preparation in the kitchen. The food is to be looked at as well as eaten. The admiration to be elicited is more, or other, than gustatory. This appeal has its own satisfactions, and it may be truly said that in Japan the eyes are at least as large as the stomachs. Certainly the number of rules involving modes and methods of presentation indicate the importance of eye appeal.

The colors, for example, must be artfully opposite. The pink of the tuna *sashimi* ought to be contrasted with the light green of the grated *wasabi* (horseradish) and the darker green of the *shiso* leaf upon which the slices rest. And the slices themselves are, despite their casual appearance, carefully arranged.

There are five types of arrangement (*moritsuke*) of food on dishes. The most common is *yamamori*, a mountainlike mounded arrangement. There is also *sugimori*, a standing or slanting arrangement, like the cedar (*sugi*) that gives the style its name. Then there is *hiramori*, a flat arrangement used for foods such as *sashimi*. And there are *ayamori* (woven arrangements) and *yosemori* (gathered arrangements) as well.

Asymmetrical aesthetics also apply in the way in which food is placed in relation to the surface area of the dish itself. Let us say something roundish—a fillet or *teriyaki*-style fish—is to be served. It will appear on a long, narrow, flat dish. Resting against the fish and extending the length of the dish will be a single stalk of pickled ginger. An asymmetrical balance has been created in which the negative space (the empty part of the dish) serves as balance to the positive (fish-filled) and is accentuated by the single line (pickled ginger), which intensifies the emptiness and, of course, by so doing also intensifies the succulence of the fish.

That such aesthetic considerations should extend to food surprises the West. One is used to Japanese concepts of negative space in such arts as *sumi-e* (black ink painting) or *ikebana* (flower arranging), but to see such ideas in the kitchen strikes us as odd—as though Poussin's ideas on the golden rectangle should be made apparent in the way a quiche is sliced.

But this just goes to show how very different Japanese ideas on food are. And there are many more aesthetic considerations common in Japanese cuisine as well. For instance, there is a general law of opposites, which has nothing in common with food presentation elsewhere. Foods that are roundish in shape (small dumplings, ginkgo nuts, small fillets) are served, as we have seen, in dishes having straight lines, while foods which are straight (square-sliced vegetables, blocks of tofu) are always served in round dishes.

At the same time, the dishes themselves are rotated during the year, because each of the four seasons calls for special ware—glass dishes, for example, are associated with summer, and bowls considered appropriate for spring could not be used in the autumn. This is particularly true for the natural containers of which Japanese cuisine is fond—seasonal leaves serving as a base on the plate, actual clam shells for seafood, and so on.

Such rotation reflects, or mirrors, the larger seasonal concern in the food itself.

The West observes season only insofar as availability and safety (no oysters in "r"-less months) is concerned. In Japan, however, the season must be reflected in all food. Even in these days of year-round fresh hothouse produce, the seasonal aspect of Japanese cuisine is kept strong.

Eggplant is best savored in summer, while spinach and other greens are considered winter fare. The only time to find and eat the *matsutake* mushroom is early autumn; trout is a spring and the troutlike *ayu* an early summer fish; and no *nabemono* (one-pot meal) is edible in the summer. The diet itself is controlled by the seasons, and the garnishes are seasonal as well. In spring, for example, a single fiddlehead may be nibbled at; in the fall, a scattering of baby maple leaves (inedible) may be found on the appropriate plate beside the appropriate food.

Whoever said Japanese cuisine was all presentation and no food was, of course, quite wrong, but one can at the same time understand how such a statement came to be made, particularly if one comes from a country where it is simply enough that food looks decent and tastes all right.

Actually, the presentational ethos so much a part of the Japanese cuisine continues right into the mouth. Is there any other cuisine, I wonder, which makes so much of texture, as divorced from taste? The West, of course, likes texture, but only when it is appropriate and never when it is tasteless. Consequently, the feel of the steak in the mouth, the touch of the clam on the tongue are part of the Western eating experience, but they are not enjoyed for their own sakes. Rather these sensations are enjoyed as harbingers of taste.

Japan, is again, quite different. There are, in fact, not a few foods that are used for texture alone. *Konnyaku* (devil's tongue jelly) has no taste to speak of though it has an unforgettable texture. *Tororo* (grated mountain yam) again has much more feel than flavor. *Udo* looks like and feels much like celery but it tastes of almost nothing at all. *Fū*, a form of wheat gluten, has no taste, except the flavor of whatever surrounds it. Yet all are prized Japanese foods.

The reason is that the Japanese appreciate texture almost as much as they appreciate taste. The feel of the food, like its appearance, is of prime importance. The West, on the other hand, does not like extreme textures. Those few Westerners who do not like sushi or *sashimi* never say that it does not taste good. Rather, it is the texture they cannot stand—the very feel of the food.

Not only do the Japanese like textures, they have turned their consideration into one more aesthetic system governing the cuisine. Textures, runs the unwritten rule, ought to be opposite, complementary. The hard and the soft, the crisp and the mealy, the resilient and the pliable. These all make good and interesting combinations and these, too, have their place within this presentational cuisine.

There are other aesthetic considerations as well but this is a good place to stop and take stock of what we have so far observed. For review let us take a very simple dish, a kind of elemental snack, something to eat while drinking, a Japanese canapé. Let us see how it contrives to satisfy the aesthetic demands of Japanese cuisine.

The dish is *morokyū*, baby cucumber with *miso* (bean paste), usually consumed with saké, more often nowadays with beer. Let us look at its qualities. First, the colors are right; fresh green and darkish red is considered a proper combination. Second, the portions are small enough so that their patterns can be appreciated—the dish consists of just one small cucumber cut up into sticks and a small mound of *miso*. Third, the arrangement and plate complement each other. The round mound of *miso* (*yamamori*) is considered operative, so the dish is served on a long, flat, narrow plate, thus emphasizing the very roundness of the bean paste. The length of the cucumber—and it is always cut along its length, never its width—stretches away from the *miso* and emphasizes the emptiness and again, by contrast, the fullness of the food. Fourth, the dish should be redolent of summer, since *morokyū* is mainly eaten in warm weather. So the dish should be untextured, unornamented, of a light color—white, pale blue, or a faint celadon green—thus emphasizing the seasonal nature of *morokyū* itself. Fifth, the textures are found to blend. The cool crispness of the cucumber complements perfectly the mealy, soft, and pungent *miso*.

Let's see, is there anything else? Oh, yes, almost forgot—the taste. Well, *morokyū* tastes very good indeed, the firm salty *miso* fitting and complementing the bland and watery flavor of the cucumber. But it is perhaps telling that, with so much going on in this most presentational of cuisines, it is the taste that one considers last. Perhaps it is also fitting. The taste of this cuisine lingers.

Naturally, one cannot compare the taste of a few slices of fresh fish and almost raw vegetables with, let us say, one of the great machines of the French cuisine, all sauces and flavors. And yet, because it is made of so little, because there is so little on the plate, because what there is is so distinctly itself, Japanese cuisine makes an impression that is just as distinct as that of the French.

This is because the taste is so fresh, because the taste is that of the food itself and not the taste of what has been done to it. The sudden freshness of Japanese cuisine captures attention as does a whisper in the midst of shouts. One detects, in presentation and in flavor, authenticity. Things are introduced and eaten in varying degrees of rawness, nothing is overcooked; one feels near the food in its natural state. Indeed, one *is* often very near it because so much Japanese food (cut bite-sized in the kitchen and arranged on plates before being brought out) is cooked or otherwise prepared at the table, right in front of you.

Japanese cuisine is, finally, unique in its *attitude* toward food. This ritual, presentational cuisine, which so insists upon freshness and naturalness, rests upon a set of assumptions concerning food and its place in life. Eventually, the cuisine itself depends upon the Japanese attitude toward the environment, toward nature itself.

These assumptions are many. First, one will have noticed that the insistence upon naturalness implies a somewhat greater respect for the food than is common in other cuisines. At the same time, however, it is also apparent that respect consists of doing something to *present* naturalness. In other words, in food as in landscape gardens and flower arrangements, the emphasis is on a presentation of the natural rather than the natural itself. It is not what nature has wrought that excites admiration but what man has wrought with what nature has wrought.

Thus Japanese cuisine is as anthropomorphic as most cuisines are, but it is anthropomorphic in a different way. Man in Japan includes the natural more than does man in other countries perhaps because the Japanese sees himself as an adapter, an ameliorator, a partner. He does not see himself so completely lord of the universe that he could design a formal Italian garden or prepare *tripes à la mode de Caen*, a dish featuring four or more kinds of tripe simmered with a cow's foot and various vegetables in the dry cider of Normandy for fourteen hours.

Certainly nothing, food included, gets into the Japanese world without becoming Japanified. This is true of other cuisines as well. Most Western food is eaten by most Japanese—eaten every day as a matter of fact—but it is changed, sometimes subtly, sometimes not—to the satisfaction of the native palate.

The Western breakfast, for example, is now very popular, particularly in the cities, but it is understood that the eggs always be sunny-side-up and served cold and that a small salad (often using cabbage) is necessary if the meal is to be authentic.

Or, there are some dishes which we foreigners think of as being completely Japanese since they occur nowhere else, for example, chicken rice, curry rice, and *hayashi* rice. Yet all are adaptations which have suffered a great change in Japan. Chicken rice is a ketchup-flavored cross between pilaf and fried rice; curry rice was obviously once Indian; *hayashi* rice was, despite its native name, perhaps once North American—*hayashi* is how the Japanese originally understood "hashed."

The Japanese, of course, think of such food as being originally imported, though it has now become in an honorary sense Japanese. Though they are omnivorous as far as cuisines go, a great distinction is thus made between the Japanese and all the others. (And not only in food. The rigid division between things Japanese and things otherwise is to be observed in all fields of human endeavor in Japan.)

Restaurants serving Japanese food, for example, serve only Japanese food and those serving Western food serve only Western food. It is only in the lowly *shokudō* (something like the Western station buffet) that the categories are mixed. (In those and in the smart avant-garde eateries among which *nouvelle cuisine* got its start, where there are such miscegenous dishes as raw tuna over avocado and pasta with sea urchin roe.) One of the reasons (there are many more) is that Japanese food Japanese-style has for the Japanese a special character, more so than does, for example, American-style American food for the American.

Though Japanese-style food is usually eaten at least once a day by all Japanese (so great are the inroads of Western-style food and now the fast and/or junk foods), it is never taken for granted the way that a Big Mac (or *Châteaubriand*, for that matter) could be taken for granted.

Rice was the food of the gods and even now the Japanese meal, centered as it is around rice, retains something of a sacerdotal character. Certainly, to be served such food (Japanese home-cooking) in someone's house is an honor. Visiting foreigners are also often steered to authentically Japanese food. (And the Japanese feel that even such landed cuisines, as, say, *tonkatsu* are not Japanese enough for such presentation.) *Real* Japanese food remains both something very homelike and something at the same time rather special.

If nowadays the home table tends to be a bit mixed (*sashimi* and salad, something sweet and sticky at the end), it is not perhaps that Japan has become so Westernized as that things Western in Japan have been so Japanified.

At the same time there exists a concern for the purity of the Japanese cuisine as it has evolved, and Japan remains one of the countries (France is another) where food represents a lineage, going back into history. Where, indeed, the cuisine is rightly viewed as one of the cultural adjuncts of the country itself. Thus, an understanding and appreciation of Japanese cuisine implies a certain understanding and appreciation of the Japanese themselves.

Edo-style *nigiri-zushi*.

SUSHI

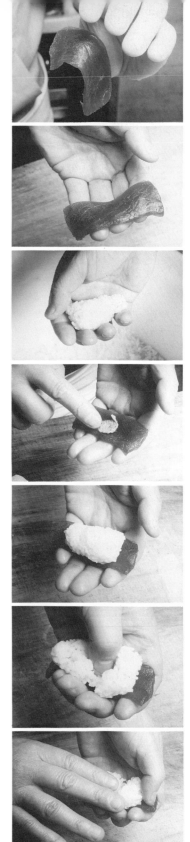

S ushi, one of Japan's most representative foods, is now fairly well-known around the world. Most large cities in Europe and the United States have sushi shops, and the dish has even been described by the *New York Times*.

Here is Craig Claiborne's definition: "An assortment of small morsels of freshest raw fish and seafood pressed into cold rice lightly seasoned with vinegar." This is a perfectly serviceable description so far as it goes, but it does not go far enough. Sushi is a delight to the eye, a revelation to the tongue, and an engrossing culinary happening that those who have partaken will not soon forget.

The sense of occasion that distinguishes sushi eating begins as soon as one walks into the shop. Behind a long counter of immaculate white cypress is a glass-cased, ice-cooled array of fish fillets and shellfish, all unmistakably fresh and some alive. This decor, colorful, crisp, offers the eye an overture of delights to come. Behind stand the sushi master and his assistants, all in white, ready to perform.

After the apprentice has brought a cup of hot tea, a small dish for soy sauce, an ice-cold *oshibori* (hand towel), and pinches of picked ginger to refresh the mouth between bites, one is ready to order.

Some prefer an hors d'oeuvre of freshly cut *sashimi* accompanied by beer or hot or iced saké. Others want to begin directly with sushi. In either event, there is the widest of choices. In order of probable popularity are *maguro* (tuna), *toro* (the marbled underside of the tuna), *chū-toro* (a half-marbled side section of the tuna), *uni* (sea urchin roe), *ebi* (shrimp, boiled or alive), *tai* (sea bream), *ika* (squid), *akagai* (ark shell), *hamachi* (young yellowtail), *buri* (adult yellowtail), *tako* (octopus), *ikura* (salmon

roe), *anago* (conger eel), *awabi* (abalone), and many other seasonal fishes and shellfish, ending up with the only nonseafood item in the lot—*tamago-yaki*, a bit of thick, slightly sweet omelet on rice.

The sushi master, upon hearing an order, gets busy with fingers and knives, and here the performance begins. Deft and skillful, each stroke swift and precise, he cuts and slices, scoops a double fingerful of rice, adds a bit of *wasabi* (horseradish), and swiftly forms the oblong ball, firmly capped by the seafood. A piece of sushi thus properly done has, it is said, all the grains of rice facing in the same direction, and acquiring this technique takes, say the masters, many years.

Two such "fingers" of sushi constitute an order. While it is all right to use the chopsticks provided, the knowledgeable do not. They pick up a piece, turn it over, and dip the seafood side lightly into the soy sauce, then convey it to the mouth. Savoring the freshness, they then regard the sushi master at work on the next order, in due time calling out their own.

Sushi was not always this delicious happening. Originally, it was nothing more than a way of preserving fish. Rice was packed around the fish fillets and then thrown away before the aging flesh was eaten. Gradually, over the centuries, this turned into *nare-zushi* (still eaten in the country), layers of fish and layers of rice in a jar with a stone on top. The rice ferments, giving the sharp sweet taste that vinegared rice now approximates.

This dish became, in turn, what is still known as Osaka-style sushi. Fresh seafood is put into a shallow mold, rice is added, and the whole is pressed. The result is a kind of large pie, which is then cut into bite-sized pieces. The more popular Edo-style finger-formed *nigiri-zushi* described above and now eaten universally, originated in Tokyo (then Edo) in the early nineteenth century. There is no fermenting, no pressing into molds, no waiting. Such sushi has been called the world's first fast food.

Having come into its own, sushi proliferated into a number of forms, all now available at the sushi shop, in addition to the finger-formed bite-sized staple. One such is *nori-maki*. A square of seaweed is swiftly coated with rice, *wasabi* is added, something is put in the middle, and the whole is rolled into a long cylinder, which is then cut into pieces or eaten as is. If the stuff in the middle is cucumber, the sushi is called *kappa-maki*; if strips of fresh tuna, *tekka-maki*; if

Forming one finger of *nigiri-zushi* is a seventeen-step process, but a good sushi master performs with such speed and precision that it all seems easy.

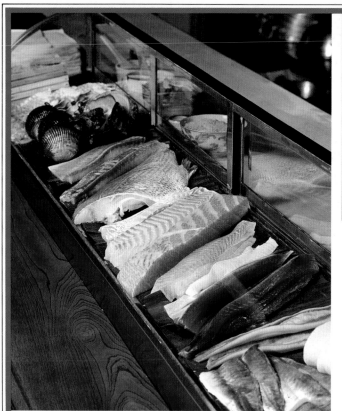

ABOVE: In addition to making perfectly formed sushi, a sushi master must establish rapport with his customers.

LEFT: A refrigerated case holds all the topping ingredients.

BELOW: Pressed sushi. (Clockwise from the upper left corner): *anago-zushi; masu* (sea trout) sushi, packed in bamboo leaves; *ōmura-zushi*, made by placing a layer of fish in the middle of the rice as well as on top and topping the whole with omelet; *kodai* (small sea bream) sushi; *kohada* (gizzard shad) sushi; *saba* (mackerel) sushi.

gourd, *kampyō-maki*. A variation of the *nori-maki* is to roll the seaweed on the bias to make an ice-cream-cone-shaped sushi—a modern development, this.

Another form is *inari-zushi*, vinegared rice packed into a bag of deep-fried tofu. Another is *sasa-zushi*, rice wrapped in dwarf-bamboo leaves. Yet another is *chirashi-zushi*, which is seafood, omelet, vegetables, etc., scattered over or mixed into rice. And there are other varieties of sushi as well.

All are distinguished by the deftness of construction and the freshness of the ingredients. The seafood must be just out of the sea. This means that the master must be an expert shopper as well. He goes to the fish market early in the morning, making the earliest and best choices. He encourages his better customers to eat no later than the midday meal, and much deplores those who supper on sushi or, worse, drop in for a late night snack. By that time the seafood is no longer fresh enough to please the discerning palate.

The discerning palate has long made much of sushi, and an entire mystique has grown around the culinary drama that sushi eating constitutes. The sushi aficionado knows the very best sushi shop—the one no one else knows about. He knows what fishes are in season and consequently freshest. He also knows the master and always asks his advice. How is the tuna today?—had he better stick with *maguro*, or might he venture to the *chū-toro*, or is today one of those fine days when he may go all the way with *toro* itself? Master and connoisseur discuss the possibilities and then, with gravity and responsibility, make the choice.

The sushi *tsū* (a word denoting a person of extreme knowledge/ability) will also of course know the proper language, since the sushi mystique insists upon a separate vocabulary. In addition to knowing all the proper names of the varieties, he will know that one does not call soy sauce *shōyu* but, rather, *murasaki*; that ginger in the sushi shop is not called *shōga* but *gari*; that *wasabi* is *sabi*; that tea is not *ocha* but *agari*; and that when he asks for the bill he does not call for the *kanjō* but the much more elegant *oaisō*.

Another element entering into the sushi mystique is its expense. Though perhaps beginning as a fast food, it has now become one of the most expensive cuisines in Japan. A meal at a first-class sushi shop

PRECEDING PAGE: Three types of *chirashi-zushi*. (From top left): *gomoku* (mixed) *chirashi*, bamboo shoots *chirashi*, shrimp *chirashi*. Often prepared at home, this form of sushi is shown served with a clear soup containing *wakame* seaweed and white fish, a trefoil and *daikon* radish salad, and flounder *sashimi*.

Genrokuzushi. In this fast-food sushi chain, the sushi is placed on small plates which go around and around on a conveyor belt, and the customer picks up what he wants. The bill is calculated by the number of plates.

Kozōzushi, Japan's largest fast-food take-out sushi chain. Shown below are *nori-maki*, *nigiri-zushi*, and *inari-zushi*.

costs much more than a full steak dinner, and everyone knows how expensive beef is in Japan. The reason is, of course, that the best shops serve the best fish, and the days are long gone when tuna frolicked in Tokyo Bay. Nowadays a fresh (not frozen) tuna at the Tokyo fish market can cost thousands of dollars, and enough *toro* to make four servings costs well over twenty-five dollars. And these prices are wholesale—without overhead and profit added.

So be prepared for something special when the sushi master totes up the bill. (This, as befitting his near-sacerdotal status, he does with expected panache: he has memorized just what every one of his twenty-so counter customers have had and with calculatorlike swiftness announces the amount.) A hundred dollars a person (25,000 yen or so) is not so unusual. In a really fine shop the bill can come to much more. One can also, however, eat fairly well for twenty-five dollars (around 5,000 yen) but do not expect superb *toro*.

The first-class shops serve only freshly caught seafood. Other shops serve seafood flown into Japan, usually frozen. Sea urchin roe is from Los Angeles, prawns from Mexico, squid from Africa, herring and tuna from the Atlantic. Some tastes survive the journey. Others do not.

There is at present a general concern in Japan about the price of sushi and the (un)availability of materials. One spokesman recently said: "With raw material costing so much, the traditional sushi industry cannot survive." The spokesman was, to be sure, connected with the traditional sushi shop's greatest rival, Kozōzushi, Japan's largest fast-food sushi chain, an organization far outdistancing such competitors as McDonald's and Colonel Sanders. It has two thousand sushi take-out outlets in Japan.

The secret of Kozōzushi is, they say, to use the best possible Japanese ingredients (they do not define "possible") coupled with American merchandising and marketing techniques. Buying in bulk, they are able to charge less per item, and mechanization cuts down on labor. And, as for the making of the *nigiri-zushi*, well "anyone can learn to make sushi in 10 days." So much for the *tsū*.

So much as well for the ambience, the skill, the dedication, and the sheer technique of sushi making at its best. Still, there are between ten and fifteen thousand sushi shops in Tokyo alone, and at least a part of the population seems willing to pay high prices in return for the complete sushi experience: taste, sight, decor, performance, bill, and all. So long as such customers survive, so will the art of sushi.

SUKIYAKI

E ven if nothing else is known about Japanese food, one will have heard of—and perhaps even eaten—sukiyaki. This beef and vegetable mixture is for many the best-known and the best-tasting of all Japanese dishes.

Roland Barthes has perhaps best described it. "Sukiyaki is a stew whose every element can be known and recognized, since it is made in front of you, on your table, without interruption while you are eating it. . . . It is the very essence of the market that comes to you, its freshness, its naturalness, its diversity, and even its classification, which turns the simple substance into the promise of an event."

Beef, thinly sliced, simmers in sauce both piquant and slightly sweet; onions, grilled tofu, *shiitake* mushrooms, chrysanthemum leaves, and other vegetables, all very lightly cooked, add their flavors, bringing to the tender beef a freshness not usually associated with meat. The taste is unique, a combination of qualities that once experienced is not to be forgotten.

In Japan, where sukiyaki is just as popular as it is in the West, the dish is classified as a *nabemono*, food cooked usually at the table in a single pot or pan, and is thought of as being a winter meal. One reason for its popularity is that sukiyaki is perhaps the easiest of all Japanese dishes to prepare well. Anyone can make it and it always tastes good, though different parts of the country have their own variations.

In the Kansai (Osaka-Kyoto) area, but increasingly in Tokyo as well, a lump of beef suet is melted in a shallow iron pan over medium-high heat (usually a gas burner at the table). Very thin slices of beef are then placed, one by one, in the bottom and allowed

LEFT: Sukiyaki, the favorite of millions.

to brown. Over these are put the other ingredients: grilled tofu, green onions or Japanese long onions cut diagonally into bite-size lengths, *shiitake* mushrooms, *ito konnyaku* (devil's tongue jelly in filaments), and so on.

The liquid is then poured into the pan. This is a combination of soy sauce, water, sugar (to taste), and *mirin* (sweet sake). Knowing just when to pour in this cooking liquid is one of the arts of sukiyaki. When all the ingredients are simmering, the *shungiku* (chrysanthemum leaves) are added.

In the meantime one is turning the meat with chopsticks and shifting the vegetables so that they cook evenly. Cooking takes very little time and when the chrysanthemum leaves go in, the meat is usually ready to eat. One must not overcook sukiyaki, and some of the ingredients, the chrysanthemum leaves for example, are scarcely cooked at all. The idea is to eat everything while it is still fresh.

During this time a raw egg has been broken into a bowl, one egg for each person. A bit of soy sauce is added if desired and the egg is then lightly beaten. This is the sauce into which the meat and vegetables are dipped before eating. Their heat congeals the egg, making a succulent coating for each mouthful.

Some prefer to eat their sukiyaki over a bowlful of white rice. Others prefer to drink saké while eating. You cannot do both. Saké is never drunk with rice. Usually, the rice is brought in later and the now well-simmered sukiyaki is (if you are home and not being polite at someone's house) put directly on the rice and eaten off it.

Sukiyaki gets better and better as the cooking progresses, some think, and find these last remnants delicious indeed. They are also caramelized if you put in too much sugar. One goes on eating long after the point of satiety is reached, and satisfied groans usually accompany the completed sukiyaki feast.

There are wide variations in cooking methods. In the Kanto (Tokyo-Yokohama) area, for example, traditionally the liquid is put into the pan first, and the meat and vegetables are added to the heated liquid, making a kind of stew. In Nagasaki, the meat is ground. In northern Honshu, sukiyaki is often made with wild boar or deer. One also hears of pork and chicken sukiyaki, but these are treated with disdain by the connoisseur. Beef is the proper ingredient and it ought to be marbled, the famous (and expensive) *shimofuri niku* where fat and lean have been massaged into a tender and uniform texture.

For a dish this well-known, there is a surprising lack of accord among the accounts of where it came from. Most Japanese think of it as being vaguely ancient. Actually, however, it seems to be recent.

The ancient theory rests insecurely upon several anecdotes. One is about a nobleman in medieval Japan. Hungry after the hunt, he stops at the hut of a humble peasant and orders him to cook the game he has bagged. Humble peasant realizes that his cooking utensils are improper for lordly food. So he cleans up his plow blade (*suki*) and broils (*yaku*) the meat on it. Another is about the carnivorous Portuguese who appeared in Japan in the sixteenth century. Meat

Making sukiyaki. This restaurant cooks the long green onions before putting in the meat. The vegetables are placed over the meat, the liquid is poured in, and finally the chrysanthemum leaves are added.

This illustration from *Sitting around the Stew Pan*, written in 1872, shows a *gyū-nabe* patron dressed in Western clothes and wearing his hair short—both marks of the modern, civilized man.

The interior of Okinatei, a Kyoto sukiyaki restaurant that has continued to serve *gyū-nabe* since it was established in 1872. The scene inside the restaurant is very like the illustration in *Sitting around the Stew Pan*.

eaters all, they were soon cutting up animals and *yaku*ing them just everywhere, even on *suki*.

One of the reasons that the Japanese would have considered such eating habits worthy of remark was that they were at this time not themselves meat eaters. Though Japan seems to have had cattle since the third century A.D., they do not seem to have been a staple of the diet. Still, someone must have been eating them, because in 676 the Emperor Temmu issued an ordinance aimed at making his people stop eating cows (as well as horses, monkeys, and chickens). He did so because by this time Japan had embraced Buddhism and its prohibitions concerning meat eating. This introduced an age of euphemism (deer was known as "mountain whale"), and the cow was not again mentioned until the middle of the nineteenth century.

In the 1860s when the country was opened to foreigners and the new Meiji emperor began his reign, the Japanese were at first appalled and later intrigued to discover that their new foreign friends were meat eaters, specifically consumers of the cow —milk, meat, and all.

It was to feed them that the first slaughterhouses were established—after the Shinto priests had been called in to purify the premises. The Japanese, after centuries of living with a taboo against meat eating, remained wary. It was soon seen, however, that the foreigners were both large and enterprising. Perhaps this had something to do with the diet. The Japanese, concerned to a man with the goal of "catching up with the West," began to look at cows with new eyes.

An example of the new regard is a popular work of the period, *Sitting around the Stew Pan*, (*Agura-nabe*), a short book written in 1872 by Kanagaki Robun. Here patrons of a beef stew shop tell their stories, most of which have to do with the desirability of eating beef. One, a geisha, has acquired a taste for beef while performing for foreigners in Yokohama. She says—in Donald Keene's translation: "Even after I got back here in Tokyo, I discovered that if I didn't eat meat once every three days, I somehow didn't feel right. The meat here (Tokyo) is very good, but in Yokohama they take freshly killed beef and stew it with carrots. Once it's really tender, I think it's the best thing I've ever eaten."

In 1873, the emperor himself was pleased to release a statement saying that "His Imperial Highness graciously considers the taboo [against meat] to be an unreasonable tradition." With this authority, one local prefecture issued an ordinance saying: "There are still many who say that beef eating is flighty and does not respect the gods. This kind of thought not only slows down the pace of civilization but also is against the Emperor's expressed wishes." Shortly after there appeared a typical Meiji period aphorism, which said: "A man who does not eat beef is an uncivilized man."

With all of this sanction, beef eating became a sudden rage. It was civilized, chic, cheap, and good. The Age of Beef was ushered in. In the words of anthropologist Naomichi Ishige: "Beef became to food what, in a comparative sense, the orgy is to sex."

And the most popular way to serve it was sukiyaki. (Still called *gyū-nabe*—the term, sukiyaki, did not enter the language, says food expert Tetsunosuke Tada, until late in the Taisho period, 1912–25.) By the end of the century such "parlors" (usually serving nothing else) were everywhere. From whence this particular recipe came will probably never be known—like the compact, economical family car, it was something that appeared to fill a need.

Alas, sukiyaki is no longer the economical dish it once was in Japan. The price of beef has made restaurant sukiyaki relatively expensive. Now that everyone, thoroughly carnivorous, wants to eat meat, few can afford it in the quantity they would like. Thus, Japan's most popular and widely known dish has become, in Japan, a delicacy.

The exterior of Okinatei.

TEMPURA

Tempura—delicately deep-fried seafood and vegetables, served hot and crisp, lacy golden on the outside, juicy and succulent on the inside—is now well-known abroad.

Perhaps the reason that so many visitors have come to know it is that, although the Japanese themselves are just as fond of it, tempura is believed to be the single dish among the many in Japan that foreigners just naturally take to.

Indeed they do, but it is interesting that the Japanese, now quite used to the *sashimi* and sushi appreciating foreigner, should still insist upon the rightness, indeed, the propriety, of these same guests being taken first to the tempura restaurant.

The reason is tempura was first introduced into Japan from abroad. It is thought to be of Portuguese origin, brought into the country by the missionaries, merchants, and sailors who first visited the country in the last half of the sixteenth century. Besides guns and the Bible they brought tempura.

The word itself is locally thought to be a Japanification of *templo*, the Portuguese for "temple." The reason given is that the Portuguese Catholics would eat only fish on Fridays and often deep-fried it. Eating the result was, thought the Japanese, a religious custom. Not knowing the Portuguese for "church," they chose the word's nearest equivalent. A most suspicious etymology. One more likely is that the word comes from *tempora*, i.e., lent.

In any event, the Japanese were already quite familiar with deep-frying. Sesame oil, used both for lamps and for cooking, was known since the eighth century. It was also apparently something of a luxury. History has recorded its price during the year 736, when it was forty-five times more expensive

than rice. History does not record what was fried, but by several centuries later the price seems to have dropped. During that period a popular dish was deep-fried rice-flour dough balls. These were called *togashi*, "Chinese cakes." At the same time the range of dishes known as *kara-age*, "Chinese fried" (fried without batter) was being developed.

Nonetheless, the Portuguese method of deep-frying seafood seems to have been a novelty, and like most novelties in Japan it shortly became quite popular. So much so that the great shogun Tokugawa Ieyasu, father of his country, is said to have died from eating, or overeating, fish tempura. Actually he died three months after a dinner of deep-fried red snapper so perhaps the causes are elsewhere. Still, the event indicates that the great had taken to this novel food. So, apparently, had the common folk. Records state that by the end of the eighteenth century the passion had spread across the land. In old Edo alone there were three or four tempura establishments for every block.

These were mainly street carts, wheeled, containing both the hot oil and the food to fry in it. It was made while you waited and was consumed immediately. Indeed, even now, one of the differences between deep-fried Western food and its Japanese counterpart is that the latter is consumed at once. Even now, in all the best tempura restaurants of Japan, you are sat in the kitchen, as it were, the chef working directly in front of you, serving the tempura as soon as it is done.

Given its foreign history, one can understand why the Japanese should think that foreigners are particularly fond of tempura. More difficult to understand is why they themselves should like it. To be sure, it tastes good and is good for you, but such qualities are usually powerless against culinary taboos and one of these in Japan is that the people do not like *aburakkoi* (greasy) food. The national preference, one is told, is for foods *assarishite iru*, that is, fresh, light, uncomplicated, barely cooked at all.

Though the problem remains if one is familiar only with the tempura served in Japanese-style restaurants abroad (all of it invariably both overcooked and greasy) a visit to a tempura restaurant in Japan itself, a good one, reveals that something deep-fried can also be as *assarishite iru* as you please.

Fine Japanese tempura, though deep-fried, is not in the slightest *aburakkoi*. It is light, grease-free, crisp, and succulent. And if you think the tempura of Tokyo is good, say those in the Kansai area, you should have it in Kyoto.

A tempura street cart. From *Kinsei shokunin zukushi ekotoba* (1805), an illustrated book by Kawagata Keisei describing the lives of shopkeepers and craftsmen.

The secret of all this freshness and lightness in a deep-fried food is in the cooking itself. Here we are far indeed from French fries and soggy onion rings and those foods doubtfully dubbed finger-lickin' good.

First, only the best and freshest materials are used. Those common to tempura include seafood and vegetables only, and the listing below gives the Japanese name as well as the translation so that you can show off in the tempura restaurant. There are *kuruma-ebi* (prawn), *shiba-ebi* (shrimp), *ika* (squid), *kaibashira* (scallop), *anago* (conger eel), *kisu* (a small fish known as sillago), *haze* (goby), *ginpō* (gunnel), and *megochi* (flathead). There are some fish which are best in certain seasons such as *shirauo* (whitebait), early spring; *ayu* (sweetfish), early summer; *yamame* (baby trout), summer; and *wakasagi* (smelt), winter. There are *shiitake* mushrooms, *ginnan* (ginkgo nuts), *shōga* (ginger), *ao-tōgarashi* (small green peppers), *fuki* (coltsfoot), *mitsuba* (trefoil), *nasu* (eggplant), and many other varieties of vegetable. There is, in fact, enough for a considerable feast.

All of this material, each portion a mouthful, is washed and meticulously dried, and is then dipped into a batter of egg and flour mixed with water. This batter is called *koromo*, which means "clothing," and there are several important, indeed crucial, things about it.

One is that ice water is used. Another is that the batter is *not* well stirred. It should be lumpy, and there should be a ring of flour around the inside of the bowl. Also, it should be made *just before* using. Any leftover batter should be thrown out and a new batch made when more food is to be fried. One of the reasons is that the batter must be filled with air bubbles, this making for a lighter texture, and only new batter contains this much air. Finally the coating should be thin rather than thick. The *koromo* should be practically see-through.

Another difference between tempura and Western deep-frying is a matter of proportion. The tempura chef says that the difference is that the West uses a thick batter and not very much oil while Japan uses a thin batter and lots of oil. The paradox is that out of all this oil comes something not oily at all.

The reason is in the oil itself. Each establishment has its own favorite (and secret) recipe, but most tempura oils are combinations in varying proportions of sesame oil and some blend of vegetable oils. All chefs agree that the temperature must be 340°–360°F (170°–180°C).

Deep-frying tempura is not easy. The temperature of the oil must be just right.

The ingredients to be fried are dipped into the batter.

Any extra batter is allowed to fall off before the tempura is fried.

The batter-coated morsels are put into this carefully temperature-regulated oil and allowed to swim about for a bit. Swim is actually what they appear to be doing, their propulsion due to their water evaporating. During this stage the chef cooks only a few pieces at a time so that the temperature of the oil is not affected. Then, at precisely the proper instant, the tempura is taken out and served.

This timing is another of the secrets of the tempura chef. He watches, looks, judges. One second, one way or the other, spells disaster. At the precise moment, the tempura a light golden brown, he plucks it out and puts it on your plate.

There are a number of variations. One of these is to create decorative and textured coatings. *Sōmen* noodles are clipped into short lengths and then scattered over the battered morsel before deep-frying. Cooked, it seems to be covered with delicate brown pine needles—hence the name of this variant: *matsuba-age*. Or *cha-soba* (green-tea-flavored buckwheat noodles) are similarly cut and sprinkled. Or *harusame* (threadlike filaments made from the Chinese green pea). None of these affect the taste of the tempura, but other batter variations do. Strips of finely chopped black *nori* seaweed or white sesame seeds mixed with almonds and cashews may be added to the batter. Such taste-changing variations are used only with certain ingredients.

The finished tempura is held over the pot to let the excess oil drain off.

Once served, the common way to eat tempura is to first dip it into a sauce. This is a delicate stock-based liquid to which grated *daikon* radish and grated ginger have been added. The true connoisseur, however, can both show his distinction and win the regard of the cook by simply lightly dipping the tempura into a small amount of table salt. This heightens but does not alter the natural flavor. Not native to old Edo, this use of salt (along with the idea of making vegetable tempura) came to Tokyo from Osaka after the 1923 Kanto earthquake—that event which put an end to many formerly regional specialties.

Proceeding through the courses (the tempura dinner is usually in courses although it is possible to order à la carte), one concludes with a sherbet or fruit—a fitting ending to a deep-fried meal which is truly light.

One serving of tempura: shrimp, *kisu*, *anago*, *megochi*, squid, small green peppers.

RIGHT: Tempura batter variations. (Clockwise from top left): *hanpen* (fish paste product) with small red shrimp and *nori* seaweed; horse mackerel with green *shiso* leaves; shrimp with *harusame*; *kisu* with *shinbikiko* (a kind of glutinous rice flour).

Ingredients for tempura. (Top tray): abalone, *anago*, shrimp, *kisu*. (Right tray): *renkon* (lotus root), green beans, ginger shoots, small green peppers, eggplant, asparagus, yam, *shiso* leaves. (Bottom tray): abalone, small scallops, shrimp, mantis shrimp, *kisu*, *haze*, squid. The top tray shows raw ingredients; the food on the right and bottom trays is ready to be fried.

TOFU

Tofu is by now the single Asian foodstuff best known to the West. The pure white cakes of soybean curd are familiar from visits to Japanese and Chinese restaurants and they now make their appearance on American and European dinner tables as well.

Tofu is one of the most protean of all foods. It can be boiled, broiled, baked, fried, steamed, marinated, dried, frozen, and eaten fresh. More can be done to it than probably any other foodstuff.

Though it has its own taste, delicate and highly prized, it also takes on the taste of whatever it is prepared with and thus serves as a base for a myriad of flavors. The taste of tofu is, as the Chinese say, the taste of a hundred things.

Tofu is, in fact, Chinese—though when it was invented is uncertain. Legend has it that a pure-minded government official thought it up during the Tang dynasty. He was so honest that he refused bribes and therefore could not afford meat. To solve his dilemma, he invented tofu, which has a very high protein content. From then on, underpaid or overly honest government staff were called "tofu officials."

The point of the story is that tofu is not only nutritious, it is also cheap. Soybeans have never cost much and the tofu-making process is inexpensive. It is simple as well.

The beans are soaked overnight in water. Then, swollen to twice their normal size, they are stone ground. Water is added to the resulting fluid, and the mixture is then boiled. It is next strained to remove the bean pulp, and the remaining liquid is soy milk.

This soy milk is often drunk as is—originally in China, where it remains a beloved beverage, and now increasingly in health-conscious Japan. When it

is heated a skin forms on the surface. This is *yuba*, also a foodstuff in both Japan and China. Dried, it keeps indefinitely.

The pulp which remains after soy milk is extracted is also eaten. Called *okara*, it is full of oil and protein and is highly nutritious though it has little flavor of its own. Now mainly used as livestock feed, it once also nourished one of Japan's greatest scholars. Arai Hakuseki, who lived during the Edo period (1615–1868), proudly related that in his impoverished student days he lived almost entirely on *okara* and that in gratitude he later, rich and famous, gave large sums of money to his charitable tofu maker.

To make tofu itself, a coagulating agent is added. Just as rennet coagulates milk into the curds from which cheese is made, so bittern, made from crude salt and containing both magnesium chloride and calcium chloride, turns soybean milk into tofu.

There are two ways of completing the tofu-making process. The first results in *momengoshi-dōfu*, ("cotton" tofu), the second, in *kinugoshi-dōfu* ("silk" tofu). To make the former, soy milk curd is put into a cotton-cloth-lined mold which has holes at the sides and bottom. The curd is weighted and this presses out the liquid, leaving the tofu firmly impressed with the cotton weave.

Although *kinugoshi-dōfu* means "silk" tofu, no such cloth is used. The name comes from the smooth and silky appearance of the finished tofu. Here the curd contains a larger amount of coagulant and is not drained. The resulting tofu tends to break more easily than "cotton" tofu and is consequently never to be cooked for a long time nor at a high temperature because it then falls apart. Though tofu recipes can use either, tofu aficionados prefer to use "cotton" tofu in such typical dishes as *yudōfu* (simmered tofu) and *hiyayakko* (chilled tofu,) because they feel that *momengoshi-dōfu*, being more traditional, is more authentic and more flavorful.

The tofu is now ready to eat. Since tofu will not keep for more than a day unless placed in water or refrigerated, the mold holding the tofu is turned upside down and put into a large vat of water where it is kept until needed.

Though the tofu-making process has become much more sophisticated (for one thing, calcium sulfate is now used instead of bittern because it makes softer tofu), this is the traditional way and is still to be seen at the shops of the some fifty thousand tofu makers in Japan. In Japan—because it was here, rather than in China, that tofu revealed its versatility.

Tofu seems to have been originally brought back

Freshly made tofu is cut into blocks and kept in cold water.

LEFT: "Cotton" tofu from Morika, a shop in Kyoto that has been making tofu for some 130 years, using soybeans produced near Kyoto and clear mountain water.

In this illustration from *One Hundred Rare Tofu Recipes* (1782), women are broiling tofu to make *dengaku*.

from China by the early Japanese envoys during the tenth century. These were mostly priests, and tofu offered a much needed dietary supplement since their Buddhist vows prevented them from eating meat. The earliest document about tofu in Japan shows that by 1183 it was fully domesticated—having been served as an offering at Kasuga Shrine in Nara. Just when it became a popular food is not known, but in later years its popularity was unquestioned.

In 1782 a book published in Osaka called *One Hundred Rare Tofu Recipes* (*Tofu hyaku chin*) became a bestseller. The following year public demand created a companion volume, *One Hundred More Rare Tofu Recipes* (*Tofu hyaku chin zoku hen*). Two hundred rare tofu recipes is impressive, a tribute to the apparently unending versatility of the foodstuff.

Atsu-age.

Kōya-dōfu.

Ganmodoki.

Unohana or *okara*. In Kyoto, this humble food is rounded into balls and sold.

Yudōfu course in a Kyoto restaurant. The course includes *yuba* tempura, simmered *hiryōzu* (known as *ganmodoki* in the Kanto area), and *goma* (sesame) tofu.

Aburage.

One of the reasons for this burgeoning was, it is said, the superiority of the Japanese soybeans, particularly those from the Yamato region—which includes Kyoto and Nara. These were supposed to be better suited for tofu making than those imported from China. Even now tofu from Kyoto is considered the finest.

Another reason was that the Japanese had begun experimenting with tofu as the Chinese never had. Even now Chinese cooking tends to regard tofu as an additive, as something which enhances something else. The Japanese, on the other hand, relish the taste of tofu itself—hence the many ways in which they prepare it.

Two of the most popular of the tofu recipes in Japan are the already mentioned summer and winter dishes. *Hiyayakko* is simply a block of chilled tofu served with grated ginger and/or chopped green onions and/or dried bonito shavings. *Yudōfu*, the winter dish, is a heated variation of *hiyayakko*. Water is poured into a clay pot into which a small piece of *konbu* seaweed has been put. Cubed tofu is added and warmed—never boiled. It is eaten with soy sauce or a soy-based dipping sauce to which the same condiments as those for *hiyayakko* have been added.

There are many other tofu recipes. *Dengaku* is drained tofu grilled with a topping made of *miso* (bean paste) flavored with sugar, saké, and sometimes sesame seeds or *kinome* leaves. *Shira-ae* are vegetables dressed with tofu. Carrot, burdock, green beans, etc., are simmered and then mixed with a dressing made from drained tofu ground with sesame seeds. *Dashi* stock, salt, sugar, and soy sauce are also added. *Iridōfu* is tofu and vegetables such as carrots, *shiitake* mushrooms, and snow peas sautéed and seasoned with saké, soy sauce, sugar, and egg. *Agedashi-dōfu* is drained tofu, dredged with potato starch and deep-fried. Over this is poured a sauce made of soy sauce, saké, sugar, salt, and *dashi* stock. It is eaten with such condiments as chopped green onions, grated *daikon* radish, and red pepper.

This deep-fried tofu is somewhat different from the similarly deep-fried tofu you get from the tofu dealers. That is *aburage*. It is made from tofu in which more coagulants have been used than in "cotton" tofu. It is cut into thin slices, press-drained, and deep-fried twice. You take it home, rinse it with boiling water to remove the excess oil, and then use it in a number of ways. Cut up, it (like ordinary tofu) is good with *miso* soups and with simmered foods. Cut open, it makes a pouch into which other foods may

Tofu making as shown in *Kinsei shokunin zukushi ekotoba* (1805). The basic process has not changed since.

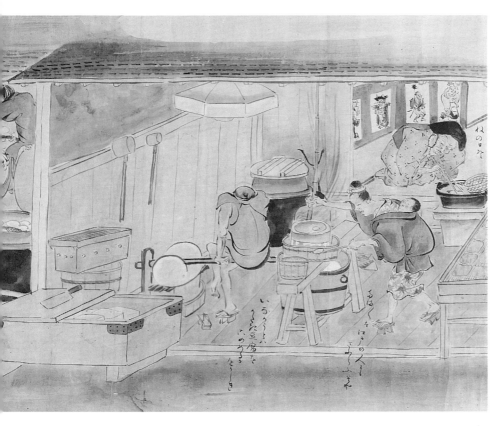

be added—the popular *inari-zushi* is made from *aburage* and flavored rice. Variations of *aburage* are the thick deep-fried *atsu-age* and the meatball-shaped *ganmodoki*.

Another way of eating tofu comes with a legend attached. Usually tofu can be kept only a day, and even refrigerated it lasts but a short time. This had long been seen as an inconvenience. Then one cold night, goes the story, in a temple at the summit of Mount Kōya, a forgetful acolyte left the tofu offering of the day on the altar. In the morning it was found frozen.

It was also discovered that this freeze-dried tofu, because it no longer contained water, could be kept for a long time, and that it could then be reconstituted by merely soaking it in water. Cooked and eaten, it was found to have a completely different texture from ordinary tofu—but one just as good. Though this tofu is known by a number of names (*misuzu, shimi-dōfu,* or *kōri-* [iced-] *dōfu*), it is also commonly called *kōya-dōfu,* after its supposed place of origin.

There are, in fact, so many different ways of preparing tofu in Japan that one can eat an all-tofu meal and come away convinced that a variegated full-course dinner has been eaten. And enjoyed—because tofu is one "health food" which is delicious.

Fugusashi looks like hundreds of petals when arranged in this chrysanthemum pattern. It is sometimes arranged to look like a crane or peony.

Fugusashi is cut so thin it is almost transparent.

FUGU

Fugu is that spiny fish that when threatened blows itself up, hence its various names of blowfish, swellfish, globefish, and puffer. Not an attractive looking creature, it is nonetheless quite good to eat when prepared as the Japanese—and the Japanese alone—prepare it.

It is served in three ways. First, the fins are toasted, put into a glass, and warmed saké is poured over them. This *fugu*-flavored drink, *hirezake*, is followed by the meat of the fish itself. It is sliced very thin and usually arranged in a floral pattern. Eaten raw, it is dipped into a sauce made of soy sauce, *sudachi* (bitter orange), chopped green onions, *daikon* radish, and red pepper. This *fugusashi* is followed by *fuguchiri*, a one-pot dish made with *fugu* and various vegetables. The meal often concludes with a rice porridge made from the remains of the *fuguchiri*. The taste is rich and meaty and contrasts well, says the aficionado, with the light and astringent *fugusashi*.

Tora-fugu, the best and most expensive of all *fugu*. The larger fish weighs almost five pounds; the smaller is not fully grown.

The names of these various dishes vary according to location. In forthright, plain-talking Osaka, *fugusashi* is called *tessa* and *fuguchiri* is called *tetchiri*. Both words have *teppo* as their root, a word which means "gun." Of *fugu* eating they say: *Ataru to, ippatsu de shinu*—If you get hit, one bullet's enough. The honest Osakan thus refers to a special property of the *fugu*. Eating it can be fatal.

The ovaries and liver can contain a very potent poison, a form of tetrodotoxin, akin it is said to curare. It is tasteless, odorless, and there is no known antidote. Someone has figured out that a grown specimen of the *mafugu* variety could kill thirty-two healthy adults.

The first sign that the guest has been poisoned is that he drops his chopsticks as his motor-nervous

The fins used in *hirezake*.

system is attacked. The alert victim will already have noticed that his mouth feels dry and that his eyes are unfocusing. These initial symptoms, occurring about twenty minutes after eating, are succeeded and concluded by a general collapse of the respiratory system. If vomiting can be induced, the life may be saved. If a person lasts half a day he will probably recover.

This being the case, one of the commoner pleasantries in the *fugu* restaurant is for someone suddenly as though accidentally to drop his chopsticks. This small clatter is followed by a deathly silence as all the other guests turn to stare and the chefs become hysterical. After it is discovered that this is a joke, there is good-natured laughter in the dining room and rueful silence in the kitchen.

The lethal properties of the *fugu* have long been known. Even around 200 B.C. Chinese scholars apparently knew about them, and Captain James Cook has written with horror about what occurred when he, against all local advice, sampled a *fugu* in New Caledonia.

In Japan, where blowfish has been eaten for centuries, this property was early known. There is an anonymous sixteenth century poem that says: "Last night, *fugu* with a friend. Today I helped carry his coffin." And the great seventeenth-century poet, Bashō, apparently had some experience as well. His haiku goes: "I enjoyed *fugu* yesterday. Luckily nothing has yet occurred."

With the lethal qualities of the blowfish so well known, one may wonder at so many continuing to eat it. One of the reasons may be that *fugu* is known (inaccurately) as an aphrodisiac. Another may be that it tastes good. Still another might be that this refined form of culinary Russian roulette is found exciting. Perhaps the main reason, however, is that its consumption is such a production that consuming *fugu* becomes a special eating treat, a kind of food happening. It is also a form of gustatorial conspicuous consumption since *fugu* is expensive.

One does not drop in to the *fugu* parlor as one does the tempura house or the sushi shop. Rather one thinks about it, then makes a reservation, then chooses the guests. Once there, the atmosphere is heightened. There is much laughter, nervous and otherwise, and when the *hirezake* appears, some are apt to observe that there is a slight numbness on lips and tongue. (This may well be quite true—a small amount of poison is found on the skin, spines, and fins.) This sensation passes, with many a remark and *frisson*, and then the banquet begins.

Fugu course. (From the top): *fuguchiri*, *fugusashi*, and the liver, which a law now prohibits serving.

In the meantime the *fugu* chefs have been preparing the meal. The liver and ovaries are carefully removed intact. Poison disposed of, the meat is then sliced. If, however, a mistake is made, there is no way for the chef to know this until the diners inform him.

Preparing *fugu* cuisine consequently requires a surgeonlike skill, and since 1949 an elaborate system of licensing has been in force, controlled by the Ministry of Health and Welfare (*Kōseisho*). The blowfish cook rarely prepares anything else, and he invariably performs with the greatest of skill. The result is that, though numbers of amateur anglers kill themselves by making *fugu* cuisine at home, no one

46

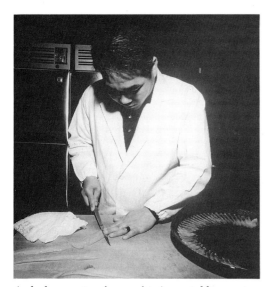

A chef preparing *fugusashi*. A special license is necessary to be a *fugu* chef, and examinations are difficult, especially in the Tokyo area.

Customers waiting for a table in a *fugu* restaurant. Reservations (and perhaps strong nerves) are required.

in the past forty years has ever been killed in a *fugu* restaurant.

Except one person. In 1975, the Kabuki actor, Mitsugorō Bandō, eating blowfish with friends, insisted upon being served the *kimo*, that is, the innards. Although the liver contains poison and is not usually eaten, it is supposed to be a great delicacy, and it is believed by some that if the preparation is perfect it is not dangerous.

In any event the point is academic, a 1984 law now forbids its being served. Only the most wayward of connoisseurs would ever have insisted upon it. This, however, apparently, the late Bandō was, the *kimo* was served, and the Kabuki actor expired.

In 1978, after an amount of deliberation due to the extraordinary nature of the case, the chef was given a suspended eight-year prison sentence and put on two year's probation. There was also an out-of-court settlement of the equivalent of about $150,000. After the actor's death a dramatic drop in sales was observed. That, however, was some time ago. The cook is perhaps again practicing, and *fugu* remains a favorite fall-winter delicacy.

It is consumed mainly in the cold months because toxicity is highest during the summer spawning

season. Consequently, as is the case with oysters, *fugu* should not be eaten in any month not containing an "r." Another reason for cold weather consumption is that it is during this season that the really big *fugu* are caught. The best is the *torafugu* (literally "tiger" *fugu*), which is striped and can weigh from three to five pounds, and be from ten to forty-eight inches in length. (Any discrepancy between weight and size is accounted for by the fact that the *fugu* is mainly air and hollow bone.) This delicious monster is found mainly in the waters off southern Honshu in Japan, near the port of Shimonoseki.

It is in Shimonoseki, therefore, that funeral rites are held yearly. Not, as might be expected, for human victims, but for the fish itself. Shinto prayers are said for the souls of departed *fugu*, and a number of caught fish are released again into the sea as a token gesture. This accomplished, the fishing boats again set forth, and their enormous hauls are happily consumed all over Japan.

Except in one special location—the imperial palace. *Fugu* is the one delicacy that the emperor and imperial family are never served. They are, in fact, constrained from eating it. Here, then, is an opportunity for the intrepid Japan traveler—the chance to eat a strange and succulent delicacy that the emperor himself has never tasted.

Fugu lanterns, often displayed at a restaurant specializing in this cuisine. The lantern is made by making a small hole in the back of a *fugu*, taking out its insides, and then drying the skin.

TONKATSU

One of Japan's most popular, and least expensive, foods is—oddly—pork. Oddly, because one does not associate this fatty animal with the general leanness of the Japanese cuisine. Chinese, yes, and Okinawan, and the fat-rich foods of Indonesia and beyond, but Japan, no. Yet the pig has definitely made a place for itself here.

It has, precisely, become naturalized. Like the cow, it was a late import, not eaten by the Japanese in any number until the latter half of the last century. Once tasted, however, it shortly became a highly popular animal.

It also had a somewhat less difficult entry. The cow had to battle a number of edicts, both religious and governmental, but the pig already had in Japan a close relative at least occasionally eaten.

This was the *inoshishi*, Japanese wild boar. Despite Buddhist precepts against meat eating, it was often consumed. An early authority, the *Teikin ōrai*, mentions that common soldiers were fond of crackling made of its skin, and there are records that somewhat later, on the first Day of the Boar in October, a kind of rice cake with young boar flesh inside was eaten. Like many forbidden delicacies (tea among them), it was enjoyed under the guise of being medicine, this particular rice cake being eaten only "to drive illness away." Likewise, from as early as the fourteenth century, both boar and deer were eaten at New Year's, but only as medicinal preparations that would enable one "to live to an old age."

Forbidden foods were also enjoyed under various euphemisms. Deer, for example, was known as *yama kujira* (mountain whale). Since the whale (*kujira*) was thought to be a fish and since Buddhist precepts said little against eating these, one might safely consume the creature, even though no whales were known to live in the mountains (*yama*). Just what sobriquet the wild boar enjoyed is not known. But the fact that it was acknowledged to be delicious and healthful certainly helped account for the early entry into Japan of its close relative, the common pig.

The form porcine cuisine took on in Japan was, however, somewhat unexpected. Since Chinese-style pork dishes were already known in Nagasaki, the major (and for centuries the only) port of entry, one might have expected pork with ginger, for example, to sweep the nation. What did in fact sweep the nation was quite different. Just as bovine cuisine took the sole form of Portuguese-influenced sukiyaki, so the single pork dish to enter Japanese cuisine became *tonkatsu*.

The name indicates the origin as European. *Ton* is a reading of the Chinese character for "pig"; *katsu* means, and indeed *is* the Japanization of the common "cutlet." Specifically, however, the original recipe seems to have been European and *tonkatsu* represents whatever the Japanese of the period could make of *côtelette de porc*.

Originally the *katsu* was beef. But during the Sino-Japanese war and the Russo-Japanese conflict which followed it, beef prices rose and pork became popular. Nonetheless, until the end of the Taisho period (1925), if you ordered a cutlet it was beef you received.

Tonkatsu itself was invented by the master of the Renga-tei in Ginza, Tokyo, a restaurant still in business. One day (in 1932 the story goes) the busy master hit upon the idea of deep-frying pork. One could make several portions at once and hence save time. Fresh, sliced cabbage, *tonkatsu*'s invariable companion, was used because it took so much less time to prepare than did cooked vegetables.

Thus, though the original inspiration might have been foreign, the result was quite Japanese. The pork, always fresh, always loin or sirloin, is cut into fillets and salted and peppered. It is then dredged in flour, dipped into beaten egg yolk, and pressed into bread crumbs. So far the process might be foreign inspired, but now the differences begin.

The major one is that the meat is cut into very thick slices, unlike the very thin *côtelette*. Another difference is that while the European cutlet is merely fried, the *tonkatsu* is deep-fried. A minimum of three inches of fresh oil is used, and the meat is immersed for from five to eight minutes or until the covering is precisely the right shade of golden brown. It is then removed from the oil, drained, and cut up into chopstick-sized pieces.

The interior of Tonki, a well-known *tonkatsu* shop in Tokyo. This shop is so popular that there are always people waiting for a seat.

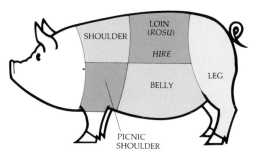

Unlike the cutlet, too, *tonkatsu* is usually thought of as a meal in itself. That is, it often comes as a set. Included is a soup, either *tonjiru*, a *miso* (bean paste) soup with pork bits and vegetables, or Japanese *miso shiru*; Japanese pickles; white rice; and sometimes fruit.

And, of course, the sauce. Even if the chef will willingly show you how he prepares the meat, he will never tell you what goes into the sauce. This is because it is a secret, and every *tonkatsu* house of any standing has its own recipe. Generally, it is made of soy sauce, saké, mustard, Worchestershire sauce, and sometimes ketchup, but the proportions are never divulged. This results in two styles: a heavy sauce which is rather sweet and a lighter sauce which is rather piquant. One does not quite know why this should be. Perhaps because pig always tastes like pig but the different sauces are unique, a "family" secret.

In any event the customer has the choice of pouring the sauce directly over the meat or dipping each portion into a small dish containing the sauce. He also has recourse to the mustard pot since this condiment is considered essential—either instead of or in addition to the sauce. There is only one other decision he must make. This is when ordering. *Tonkatsu* comes in two styles. *Rosu* (though this happens to mean lean when beef is ordered) means that an amount of fat is left, and *hire* means that the meat is entirely lean fillet. Otherwise, all decisions are left to the chef, and the *tonkatsu teishoku* (really the only proper way to eat the food) comes complete, as a set, a full meal which is delicious and (given Japan) surprisingly inexpensive.

An ordinary *tonkatsu teishoku* will cost only the equivalent of five to seven dollars at most ordinary *tonkatsu* shops. If extraordinarily good meat is used, the price will be slightly higher, but it never reaches the insane extremes of sukiyaki. Like this popular beef dish, however, it comes in only two varieties: good and very good.

So good that foreign visitors, used to greasy pork in the West, often cannot believe that it is truly pig they are eating. As an adopted and adapted cuisine, *tonkatsu* has, in this sense, achieved a kind of perfection.

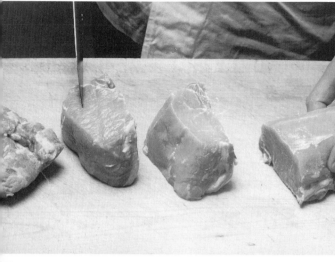

First the chef cuts the meat into seven-ounce slices. Then he pounds the meat and salts and peppers it. He dredges the meat with flour, dips it into egg, and finally coats it with bread crumbs. The chef fries it in hot oil (350°F), skimming the surface periodically, and tests it for doneness by pressing it between his fingers. He drains the oil from the finished *tonkatsu*.

Tonkatsu teishoku. The meat here is *hire* (lean) and the soup is *tonjiru*.

MENRUI

Though not perhaps a cuisine in the sense of sushi and tempura, the varieties of noodles found under the rubric of *menrui* are so good, so popular, and so Japanese that they deserve a special place in any listing of the culinary pleasures of the country.

Japanese *menrui* dishes, noodles all, come in a great variety of shapes and sizes. Further, there are numbers of different ways of serving them. Finally, this is one of the foods (sushi is another) about which the Japanese have constructed a mystique, a connoisseurship about which only the *menrui* aficionado knows.

First, the varieties. There are a great many—so many that this account will confine itself to the two most popular types: the wheat-based noodles which are associated with Osaka and the south of Japan, and buckwheat-based noodles, associated with old Edo, now Tokyo, and the north of the country.

Wheat-based noodles come in a variety of shapes, and all contain wheat flour, salt, and water. *Udon*, the best known, comes either round, square, or flat; *kishimen* is much like *udon* but is wide and flat; *hiyamugi* is round and very slender and is served cold; *sōmen* is even more slender and a bit of vegetable oil has been used in the preparation. There are also variations: *tamago sōmen*, for example, uses egg yolk among its ingredients.

The Edo buckwheat noodle, *soba* (made of buckwheat mixed with ordinary wheat), comes in a single variety: long, thin, and gray-brown in color (almost all wheat-flour noodles are white). There are, however, variations. One of the most popular is called *cha-soba* because *cha* (green tea) has been used in its preparation. In both varieties the dough is

Hot water is mixed into flour and the resulting dough is quickly kneaded. The dough is formed into a ball to keep it from drying, flattened to an even thickness, then rolled out. Using the rod, the dough is folded and cut to make the noodles.

A chef's knife is a very important tool and is well taken care of. The top knife is over 200 years old, the next dates from the Meiji period, the third from the Taisho period, and the bottom one from the present period.

Zaru soba.

Kitsune soba.

Tsukimi soba.

Tempura soba.

Tori nanba soba.

Nabeyaki udon. Udon cooked and served in an earthenware pot.

Sōmen, a favorite *menrui* for summer.

The famous *rakugo* master, Kosan Yanagi-ya, "eats" *soba* as part of his comic monologue. Since props are not used in *rakugo*, fans are used to set the scene and create atmosphere. Here they are used as chopsticks. His other hand is cupped as if holding a dish containing dipping sauce.

kneaded much more than is the case in the making of, say, Italian pasta. This is because, unlike European dough, the Japanese contains little gluten.

There are many different ways of serving *menrui* using both *udon* and *soba* and all of their variations. To the inexperienced foreigner all these may appear much alike—a noodle is a noodle. To the experienced diner however, there are many, and major, differences. The difference between Kansai (Osaka-Kyoto) *udon* and Kanto (Tokyo-Yokohama) *soba*; the differences in their dipping sauces—Kansai uses bonito and kelp stock with a light soy sauce while Kanto uses only bonito stock and a dark soy sauce. Many of the standard ways of serving these noodles, however, may use either *udon* or *soba*.

A famous dish is *tori nanba udon/soba*, the *udon* cooked with portions of *tori* (chicken) and leek, Nanba being an Osaka district famous for the excellence of this vegetable. *Ankake udon/soba* is made with noodles, green onions, *kamaboko* (fish-paste cakes) and *an*, a form of starch. *Kitsune udon* is made of *aburage* (deep-fried tofu) and onion. *Tsukimi*, literally "moon-viewing," *udon/soba* is a dish in which the noodles form the clouds and a raw egg on top provides the moon. There are also many other recipes. *Udon* or *soba* is served with tempura laid on top, for example, this combination having been for some reason decided appropriate. The most popular of the variations, however, is *zaru soba*, cold, strained noodles dipped in a piquant sauce containing chopped green onions and perhaps a touch of *wasabi* (horseradish). The simplest way to serve *menrui* is *kake* which is just noodles, broth, some chopped green onions sprinkled on top, and powdered red pepper added to taste.

There are two ways of eating *menrui*—in soup or alone with a dipping sauce. There are many variations here as well. *Sōmen*, for example, is often served in ice water. In all cases, however, the noodles are well cooked, a bit past what the Italians would consider *al dente*.

There is only one way of eating them properly, however, and that is to make as much noise as possible. Though all other Japanese food should be consumed in silence, *menrui* ought to be slurped and smacked over. One of the reasons might be that such activity somewhat cools the hot noodles, but there must be others since cold noodles are consumed just as noisily.

One reason sometimes offered is that *menrui* was originally a definitely low-class food. It came, as did all varieties of noodles, both the Korean and the Italian, from China. Indeed, the most popular form of *menrui* in Japan is not "Japanese" at all. Called *rāmen*, it flaunts its direct Chinese origin and is still, unlike *udon* and *soba*, considered a low-class food. In any event, goes the theory, the lower classes are noisy, and consequently, even now that *udon* is served in elegant establishments, it is consumed in its original, highly audible manner.

Whatever the validity of the theory, the practice is universal. Just as other Japanese cuisines must be eaten in silence, so *menrui* ought to be consumed with a maximum of noise. Otherwise, appreciation is not being shown. Here is where connoisseurship enters—knowing things like this.

The *menrui* connoisseur knows a lot. He knows, for example, that cold *soba* is eaten with very little dipping broth, the less the more elegant. And, if he is a true aficionado, he even knows the reason. In seventeenth-century Edo, during the period when *menrui* were becoming popular, it was deemed countrified to drown the noodles in the sauce. The result is that cold *soba* is, in the proper establishment, now served

Menrui. (From left): *kishimen*, a kind of thin, flat *udon*; *nagasōmen*, long *sōmen*; *cha-soba*; *soba*; three kinds of commonly used *sōmen*; *udon*; *nyūmen*, a kind of *sōmen* to be served hot; *shiraga sōmen*, extra thin *sōmen*; *sōmen fushi* (The finished noodles are hung over rods to dry; these curly segments are what remains when the noodles are cut into strips.).

Freshly made *soba*. When the dough is cut into thin noodles, it curves, producing waves.

Toshi-koshi soba. Soba restaurants stay open late on New Year's Eve to serve this dish. Its popularity is so great that without a reservation, you may not get a seat.

Muneage (roof-raising) *soba.* The roof is one of the first parts to be built in a Japanese house, and when it goes up, the newcomers invite their neighbors-to-be to have *soba* on the site. This custom is similar to that of *hikkoshi soba*, giving gifts of *soba* to one's new neighbors.

drained on flat bamboo baskets and a small amount of sauce is flavored and reserved for some dipping, if at all. In this way the connoisseur may savor the taste of the noodles themselves, flavor undiluted by an excess of sauce.

The aficionado knows that *soba* is very much a part of old Edo culture. It became *iki* (smart) to imitate the lower classes with their fast *soba* lunches—lots of noodles but very little sauce. Even now the remnants of Edo culture include *soba*—for example, *rakugo* comic monologues are full of noodles.

The connoisseur also knows the lore that has grown up around *menrui*. He is quite conversant, for example, with the even now wide-spread custom of eating *soba* as the final item on the New Year's Eve supper. He knows that this dish is called *toshi-koshi* (literally, "year-passing"), and that it, for some reason, symbolizes, as the name indicates, the old year's passing.

He is quite familiar with other *menrui* lore as well. For example, when one moves into a new neighborhood one is supposed to make gifts of *soba* to the neighbors on either side of and directly in front of one's new house. This is because (the Japanese taking an incurable delight in word play) *soba* is homonymous with *soba* meaning "near" or "next to." There is further symbolism as well. *Soba* is *hosokute nagai*, that is, narrow and long. Thus neighborly relations should be of long duration but at the same time "narrow"—they should be circumspect, discrete; the neighbors should not be continually in each other's laps.

The connoisseur also refuses to have anything at all to do with a form of *menrui* now so popular that it has, it would seem, quite taken the place of rice in the national diet. This is the prefab (just add hot water and serve) noodle which is called *insutanto*, or instant. Coming in dried, packaged form (either packet—boil for three or four minutes—or, yet more handy styrofoam cup), the instant noodle has reached the darkest corners of Japan during the twenty years since it became available, and is now ubiquitous.

Everywhere, that is, except the table of the connoisseur. Indeed, he will not touch factory-made noodles and will patronize only those establishments where the noodles are made fresh daily.

There, surrounded by those equally knowledgeable, he will—either as meal or as snack—partake of freshly made noodles, slurping and splashing, content in his knowledge, at home in his surroundings, enjoying one of the most distinct of all the tastes of Japan.

UNAGI

The taste of *unagi*, eel prepared in the Japanese manner, is indistinguishable from its texture. Flaky, charcoal-broiled on the outside, it is succulently white within. The texture of the meat, less firm than chicken breast, more firm than white fish, dissolves while the broiled outside lends a chewy consistency. The taste is, fittingly, the mildest sweet and sour with a lingering aftertaste of something slightly smoky, yet at the same time intensely natural. The contrast of the textures, the piquant aroma, the fresh warmth of the first bite, the lingering deliciousness—these complete a culinary experience that is unique. If tastes may be compared, then Japanese *unagi* might remind one of steamed carp dressed in the Chinese style, or fresh trout in the *nouvelle cuisine* manner, but the differences are just as great as the similarities. *Unagi* reminds only of itself.

Though eel is classified among the fatty meats, there is nothing fatty about this combination of texture and taste. Rather, it is decidedly lean. It tastes of protein, and indeed, eel contains more protein than do like portions of either pork or beef, in addition to fewer calories. What fat existed is distilled away in the Japanese method of cooking it. It is never stewed, nor made into soups as it is in Europe. Rather, it is steamed, then slowly broiled, and while cooking, is brushed with a mixture of soy sauce and *mirin* (sweet sake), the slightly astringent mixture which gives the dish its typical taste and aroma.

There are many ways of serving eel—all of the grilled dishes falling under the heading of *kabayaki*. Among these the most elegant is serving the best eels grilled in a lacquered box, all by itself—the rice, soup, and pickles being served separately. This is

This man prepares *unagi* in an Edo-period ukiyo-e by Yoshitoshi.

A woman prepares *unagi* in this Edo-period ukiyo-e on a fan by Yoshitoshi.

often called *kabayaki* though the word itself is a generic description.

Almost as good, and somewhat less expensive, is *unajū* which is *unagi* served in a *jūbako* or lacquered box. This is the better cuts of eel laid on a bed of rice. Its origins go back to nineteenth-century Edo where a well-known theater owner, one Ōkubo Imasuke, liked eel so much that he ate it every day. Back then cooked eel was kept warm in rice bran but taking it out was a bother, until Ōkubo hit on the idea of substituting hot rice for hot bran. One could then eat everything.

Less expensive yet is the *unagi donburi*, eel served over rice in a bowl. Its origin also seems to be theatrical. The owner of the Nakamura-za, Edo's most popular Kabuki theater, hit upon the idea of serving *unagi* directly on bowls of hot rice, making a kind of hot open sandwich that patrons could hurriedly eat between or during scenes of the play.

Both the *unajū* and the *unadon* (*unagi donburi*) have the resulting sauce poured directly over the eel and consequently over the rice as well and both are served with the herbal pepper, *sanshō*, which the patron himself sprinkles.

Both are also served with *kimosui*, a clear soup made of the liver of the eel. Or, if you want, the liver is also broiled (*kimoyaki*) and brought to the table. This liver is known as a prime health food but it is not to all tastes.

There are many other ways of cooking and serving eel besides those listed above. There is *mizore-ae*, which is blanched eel dressed with vinegar and served with soy sauce, grated *daikon* radish, and cucumber. Then there is *uzaku*, broiled eel and cucumber dressed with vinegar, soy sauce, and sugar. There is also *yahata-maki*, a grilled eel roll with sliced burdock inside. Then, there is *maki-tamago*, rolled eel-filled omelet served with *daikon* radish and soy sauce. And there are more ways beside.

Some of these are regional specialties, and, in fact, eel is served in various ways about the country. It is even dressed differently. The Kanto (Tokyo-Yokohama) style has the cook cutting from the back and taking off fins, head, and tail. The fillets are cut in two, and each is skewered and broiled skin-side down. The broiled eel is then steamed to take out leftover oils and to soften the flesh. It is then broiled again, brushed with the sauce made of soy sauce, *mirin*, and sake.

The Kansai (Osaka-Kyoto) style is different. The eel is cut from the front and fins, tail, and head are left on. It is then skewered (Kansai traditionally uses metal skewers, Kanto, bamboo) and broiled flesh-side down while the soy sauce and *mirin* mixture is brushed on. It is said that the Kanto style *kabayaki* is lighter and that the flesh is softer. The Kansai *unagi* fancier says that the tail is particularly good. Both areas agree that the eel should not be too large, though the Kansai style uses only eels over five and a fourth ounces (150 grams) in weight.

Though eels can become quite large, the Japanese feel that such eels can yield only coarse meat. Thus, if an eel is over two feet long it is usually not charcoal broiled. Rather, it is slowly steamed or grilled with salt, both operations which refine the texture. Nor are the Japanese equally fond of such eel-like creatures as *anago* (conger eel) or *dojō* (loach). While both are eaten, the prospect does not excite nor delight as does the opportunity for eating *unagi*.

The eel is eaten during all seasons in Japan but it is particularly relished during the heat of summer. Why this should be is unknown, but the association is an ancient one. In the eighth-century poetry collection, the *Manyoshū*, there is an exchange of verses in which one gentleman says that since summer heat makes one slim, eels should be eaten to keep up one's strength. To this, the other gentleman replies that he is at least alive, not yet having drowned in an attempt to catch the nourishing delicacy.

It was perhaps with this classical reference in mind that an eighteenth-century eel-shop keeper asked the then well-known natural history writer, Hiraga Gennai, to write a slogan for his shop. Since it happened to be the Day of the Ox, a zodiacal event occurring at the height of the long hot spell after the rainy season, Gennai wrote: "Today is the Day of the Ox." Patrons, knowing that the famous Gennai had written the slogan, thought there must be some deep and important connection between the Day of the Ox and eels. Such is the prestige of learning in Japan that people crowded into the shop.

Even now, on the Day of the Ox the eel restaurants of Japan are filled. Perhaps it is true that the wriggling eel thus lends us its vitality or perhaps it is just that the Japanese are pleased to have an extra reason to consume a favorite delicacy.

There is a further, if minor, reason for the popularity of the *unagi*. This is that eating it considerably improves the love life. The very shape of the creature may be one of the reasons for the association, but as a matter of fact, eel is extremely rich in vitamins A and E, those associated with reproduction. To what extent *unagi* really contributes remains unmeasured,

In this Tokyo *unagi* shop, a man prepares eels much in the same way as the man and woman in the ukiyo-e. The sign behind him gives the two Days of the Ox in the long hot spell after the rainy season when Japanese find *unagi* especially appealing.

The *unagi* are pierced with bamboo skewers and fanned as they are grilled in this Tokyo shop.

Unagi donburi, served with pickles and herbal pepper.

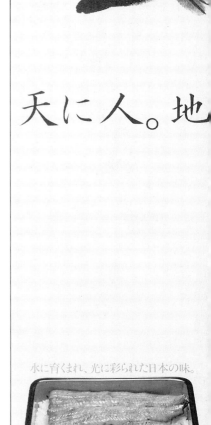

水に育くまれ、光に彩られた日本の味。

but *kabayaki* is still sometimes served the newly married couple for their morning-after breakfast.

Whatever the reason, eel is extremely popular in Japan, so much so that the country is always running out of *unagi*. In 1980 Japan consumed some 75,000 tons of it. Of this, the Japanese themselves only produced about 50,000 tons. The rest had to be imported.

One of the reasons that the native product rarely meets the demand is, of course, that nowadays many more Japanese can afford *unagi*. Another is that eels are extremely difficult to farm. And one of the reasons for this is the mystery of their life cycle.

Their very intricate reproductive habits insist that the adults migrate in order to couple. Atlantic eels go all the way to the Sargasso Sea. Where the Pacific eels go is still a mystery. The fecundated eel then returns (often to the very same river or stream, says folk wisdom), there to spawn a large number of elvers which in turn grow up to repeat the cycle.

The mishaps that eels are prone to on such a long journey much reduce the number returning. The newborn elvers have a number of natural predators and, in addition, many bays and rivers in Japan are polluted to the degree that an eel will not last long. And among the natural predators are, of course, the Japanese themselves. They consume so much eel that the three thousand eel restaurants in Tokyo alone are always running out.

One of the solutions has been massive eel farming in Japan, the largest establishments being those

LEFT: This advertising poster combines an old print of an *unagi* shop and a plate of grilled eel.
BELOW: Here an ink painting of an eel has been combined with *unajū* to produce a mouth-watering poster.
RIGHT: Eels are raised near Hamamatsu. Famous for its eels, this area also sells a pastry-like confection called "eel pie," which lists powdered eel as one of its ingredients.

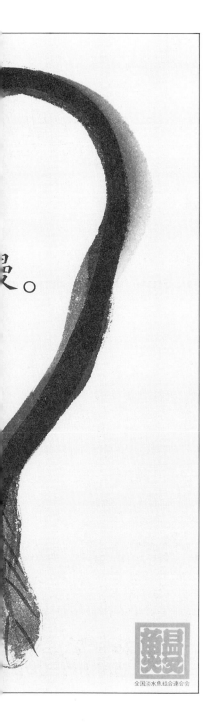

around Lake Hamana near Hamamatsu. Elvers, which the Japanese call *shirasu*, are here nurtured, kept from migrating, and consumed either when they turn a silverish color, which means that they are adult, or when they are still an adolescent yellow. The elvers themselves, however, are largely imported—usually from Taiwan, an island that has a large and stable eel population as yet undisturbed by pollution.

Another solution is to keep up eel prices so that it remains a delicacy and does not become an everyday food. Actually, more than enough *unagi* could be imported from Taiwan and Southeast Asia with the result that prices would drop. This, however, is not something that the eel-growers association desires. Several years ago, when the price threatened to lower, representatives visited the Ministry of Interior Trade and Industry and complained. Imports were promptly curtailed, and eel remained the somewhat expensive delicacy that it ought to be.

The reason it ought to be is that something this succulent should not be sullied by habit and daily consumption. A dish this delicious, this nutritious, this altogether delightful, ought to be kept for a special occasion—the Day of the Ox or not.

Unagi being grilled over charcoal. The heads are attached, Kansai style.

ONIGIRI

Rice is, of course, basic to the Japanese diet. It is the bread and potatoes of the national cuisine. Like these staples it is also capable of great variation. There are at least as many ways to serve rice as there are to prepare potatoes.

At the same time there are many differences in attitude toward these basic foods between Japan and the West. In Europe and America bread or potatoes are considered accessories, important but not indispensable. In Japan, however, rice is the core of the meal, despite what comes before or after. Without it, the Japanese, no matter how otherwise stuffed, declare that the meal was *nandaka mono tarinai*, somehow not enough. Indeed, the words for cooked rice, *meshi* and *gohan*, have come to mean the meal itself.

A consequence of this attitude toward rice—one quite different from attitudes in the West where a meal consisting of only bread or potatoes would be considered a hardship—is that the Japanese are occasionally quite happy to make a meal of *meshi* alone.

Well, almost alone, because something is usually added to provide flavor since cooked rice has little of its own. Still, no matter what is added, nor how much of it, rice itself is considered the meal.

Take, for example, the rice ball, variously called *onigiri* or *omusubi*, which itself is considered the meal. It is to be found everywhere, in stores and shops selling the newly made, hand-formed (*onigiri*) rice ball, and at parks and playgrounds, where you can see people munching on this hand-held food.

They have been doing so for a long time. The *Murasaki Shikibu Nikki*, the diary of the Lady Murasaki, author of the famous *Tale of Genji*, writes of people eating rice balls during her time, the elev-

enth century. Rice was then something of a luxury since the common people contented themselves with millet. The nobility and their officials were pleased to consume the rice balls, which were called *tojiki*, often as an alfresco repast, or as an out-of-doors picnic lunch.

The idea of eating *onigiri* outside still persists and the majority of rice balls consumed in today's Japan are enjoyed on park benches, lawns, or on real picnics. Perhaps the idea originally was that since rice balls are so portable they make ideal travel food.

Their portability also perhaps accounts for their variations. The most common rice ball is the *nori musubi*. Since *nori* is seaweed and *musubi* is another name for *onigiri*, the result is a highly portable package, a rice ball wrapped in a square of edible seaweed.

Equally popular is the *umeboshi no onigiri*, or pickled plum rice ball. Since rice not eaten shortly after cooking may go bad, the preservative *umeboshi* keeps the rice fresh during the journey. In addition, the pickled plum is supposed to be good for the health—it is recorded as having cured Emperor Murakami in the tenth century. From what ailment is not specified, but the high citric acid content does aid digestion. In any event an *umeboshi* imbedded in the center of a rice ball has long been a Japanese favorite.

The rice ball is considered a full meal in Japan in the way that slices of bread and pieces of potato would not be in the West. Perhaps the reason is Japan's feeling for rice. It is given a nearly sacerdotal status, a true "staff of life." Though this attitude is steadily eroding, it still maintains to a sometimes surprising degree.

The Japanese meal is often a big bowl of rice and several smaller dishes of things to eat with it. The *onigiri* is a portable version of this. Things to eat with it are outside (seaweed, for example) or inside (pickled plum, for instance) but the main thing is the rice ball.

This is also the structural principal behind Japan's other portable meal, the *obentō* (lunch/picnic box): a lot of rice (about half the box) and lots of small portions of other things.

Though most urban workers and school children no longer carry an *obentō*, these packaged meals remain popular. They are sold many places, but the visiting foreigner is perhaps most familiar with the *eki-ben*, those *ben* (*bentō*) sold on trains or in stations (*eki*).

No train trip of any duration is complete without an *eki-ben*. Nicely wrapped, coming complete with

Obentō have been popular for a long time in Japan as this pre-Edo-period painting shows.

Onigiri. (From left): Plain; with black sesame; wrapped in *nori* seaweed. Perhaps half the pleasure of *onigiri* is guessing what is inside.

Maku-no-uchi bentō. This rather lavish *bentō* has small portions of a large variety of things and rice shaped into fans.

chopsticks, it is opened to reveal rice in one half, other compartments containing a variety of bite-sized foods: chicken, fish, *daikon* radish, *shiitake* mushrooms, squid, salmon, mountain vegetables—and pickled plums.

Each district of Japan has its own distinctive *eki-ben* with local specialties packed inside, and one of the joys of travel in the country used to be leaning out the window to buy yet another regional *obentō*: *unagi* (eel) *meshi* at Hamamatsu, *tai* (red snapper) *meshi* at Shizuoka, and *shūmai* (Chinese dumplings) at Yokohama. This particular pleasure is now somewhat curtailed since the majority of trains are airconditioned, the windows no longer open, and schedules do not allow time for shopping on the platform. The *eki-ben* are, however, still quite available. After each major station stop, girls appear with pushcarts in the aisles of the train, each cart containing various *bentō* from the region through which one is passing. All are good, and each *eki-ben* is time-marked and sold only up to four hours after time of preparation.

The modern *eki-ben* are perhaps the descendants of the aristocratic traveling *bentō* of the Edo period.

TOP LEFT: *Kurisansai bentō* (chestnut/mountain vegetable), Aizu-Wakamatsu station, Fukushima Prefecture. This *eki-ben* retains the traditional shape, separating the rice from the other elements. TOP RIGHT: *Unagi meshi*, Hamamatsu station, Shizuoka Prefecture. CENTER LEFT: *Shūmai bentō*, Yokohama station. Yokohama has a large Chinese population. CENTER RIGHT: *Kyūbi-zushi*, Kuroiso station, Tochigi Prefecture. Among its contents are *inari-zushi*, *nori-maki*, smoked salmon, and Chinese-style roast pork. BOTTOM LEFT: *Tōge no kamameshi*, Yokokawa station, Gumma Prefecture, one of the most famous *eki-ben*. Rice, vegetables, chicken, and chestnuts cooked in a ceramic pot are sold with pickles. BOTTOM RIGHT: *Kodai suzume-zushi* (small sea bream sushi), Wakayama station.

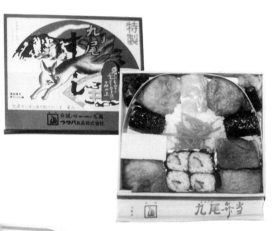

The front of Hokka-hokka-tei, a fast-food chain selling hot *bentō*. It is common to see people lined up and waiting at these shops at noon.

Picnic journeys and short sightseeing jaunts were accompanied by the most elaborate of lunch boxes, all lacquered and tiered, and containing the most delicate and expensive of foods.

Even now there are caterers who specialize in these lacquer-boxed *bentō* deluxe. One can order a *hanami bentō* to be taken along while cherry-blossom viewing. Or one may have a *maku-no-uchi* (between the curtains) *bentō* delivered to arrive between the acts at Kabuki.

One of the appeals of these rice-plus meals, *bentō* and *onigiri* alike, is that they gratify the Japanese desire to have all the food at the same time. There are no courses in the Japanese home-style meal; it is all there, in front of you. So it is in the *bentō* and so it indubitably is in the rice ball.

Another appeal might well be the look of the food. There is a promising solidity, a fullness about the rice ball. It seems a paradigm of its own qualities—a hearty heaviness, a succulent moistness, and it is quite apparently nutrient-filled: it *looks* good for you.

Onigiri are sold in many Japanese restaurants, and at the *izakaya* (Japanese-style pub) you can have a rice ball after you have finished your saké. Or—and this is one of the charms of *onigiri*—you can simply buy them at one of the many rice ball/lunch box stores or in the foods section of the department store.

Purchases complete, one settles on a park bench, riverbank, or grassy bluff, opens the bag, takes a bite, and enjoys a typical authentic taste of Japan.

Toasting *mochi* over charcoal.

MOCHI

One variation of rice, *mochi* (rice cake), is so different that it merits a chapter of its own. *Mochi* is made of glutinous rice, *mochi-gome* (the other rice, that served at the table, is the non-glutinous *uruchimai*), and it is regarded as, if not a separate cuisine, a unique and special food.

The *mochi-gome* is cooked and pounded into a paste while still warm. Much is made of the pounding, *mochi tsuki*, which is done with a huge wooden mortar and large wooden mallet. It in fact becomes a seasonal ceremony, and many are the pictures in the local press showing famous sumo wrestlers, screen and TV stars, and a number of aspiring politicians taking turns at wielding the mighty mallet.

The season is New Year's, when people all over the world but particularly, somehow, the Japanese, have the opportunity of starting over again, fresh, pure.

Mochi cakes are indeed associated with purity and are, to this extent, sacred. One of the New Year's decorations is the big, round, pure white *mochi* cake, stacked on view at shrines or in the home during this season. These cakes are called *kagami mochi* and are named after the mirror (*kagami*), which is one of the three sacred treasures of Japan, the other two being the sword and the jewel. The rice cake is the essence of sacred rice itself, its spirit or soul. Traditionally the Japanese have thought themselves quite near their gods. Food and drink is put on the family altar in the main room of the house. After the New Year's has passed, Japanese even now eat the *kagami mochi* which has been offered to the gods. In this case the spirit of the rice, enriched as it were by the gods, is happily ingested.

All of this is much supported by folklore. One of the oldest legends concerning *mochi* is that a wealthy

man once hung a mirror-shaped rice cake as an archery target—fitting, one would think, in that its shape was also that of the bull's-eye target. Not at all. With the first arrow the *kagami mochi* suddenly turned into a great white bird and flew away—carrying with it, of course, all of the rich man's fortune. The gods do not countenance disrespect.

There are many connections between *mochi* and money. During the feudal Edo period the shogun gave rice cakes to doubtless disappointed daimyo, in lieu of monetary offerings previously proffered. When the notoriously avaricious shogun Tokugawa Ieyasu, traveling by the Abe River, was struck by the appearance of the local *mochi*, rice cakes covered with powdered *kinako* (soybean flour), he was told by the *mochi* seller that the powder was really gold dust. Ieyasu consumed a number on the spot. This variety is still called Abe River *mochi*, and many are the tales of its money-bringing possibilities.

When Japanese children look at the moon, that *kagami-mochi*-shaped object, they see not a man but a rabbit. And what is that felicitous animal doing? He is pounding *mochi*. Look, see the mortar, see the pestle? If one succeeds in so seeing, one's good fortune is assured for yet another year. The rabbit, thrifty beast, is one of the few in Japanese folklore that never goes hungry.

Nonetheless, at one point in Japan's history this rage for the good fortune brought by *mochi* appears to have threatened Japan's economy. There is record of Prince Shōtoku, back in the eighth century, stopping the making of rice cakes because it encouraged extravagance. People were buying *mochi* instead of other foods. Other businesses were complaining. Nevertheless the popularity of *mochi* was such that the edict was not long efficacious. There are many *mochi* references in later Japanese history and literature as well, a famous one being the *kagami mochi* mentioned during a description of a wedding ceremony in *The Tale of Genji*.

All this talk of felicity reminds one, of course, of China, and *mochi* is almost certainly a Japanese importation from that country. Historically, it seems to have come—very early—through Korea from the province of Yunnan on the Chinese mainland. It is still a local specialty there, and the *mochi*-like rice cake in its various forms is found in southern China, Sri Lanka, Thailand, Burma, and perhaps a few other countries as well. It is, however, nowhere other

Sumo wrestlers pounding *mochi*, a familiar sight around New Year's. One wrestler pounds the *mochi*, and one turns it.

TOP: *Isobe-maki.*
BOTTOM: *Kurumi-zenzai* (left). Puréed walnuts and tofu are poured over grilled *mochi*. *Oshiruko* (right). Cooked and sweetened red beans are poured over grilled *mochi*.

LEFT: *Ozōni.* Without *ozōni*, it just wouldn't be New Year's. The top photograph is Kyoto style, the lower is Kanto style.

than in Japan made so much of, and nowhere else does it come in so many varieties.

Since *mochi* is simply pounded rice, one might think that there is not much one can do with it. One would be wrong. Japan's ingenuity in transforming the simple and the homely into something completely other is nowhere better exemplified than in what the Japanese do with *mochi*.

There is, first, plain white *mochi*, a cake that is toasted and served with soy sauce and sometimes sugar. This is standard New Year's food, but it is eaten at other times of the year as well. Then there is *isobe-maki* which is toasted *mochi* dipped in soy sauce and wrapped in seaweed; *karami mochi*, which is freshly pounded rice cake mixed with grated *daikon* radish and soy sauce; the previously mentioned *abekawa* (Abe River) *mochi*, which is freshly pounded or toasted *mochi* coated with *kinako* and sugar; *zenzai*, which is freshly pounded *mochi* and sweetened red beans; *shiruko*, *mochi* in a sweet purée of red beans, and so on.

The shape varies. In the Kansai (Osaka-Kyoto) area, individual round cakes are made. In the Kanto (Tokyo-Yokohama) area, rectangular sheets of *mochi* are cut into square pieces.

In addition, the rice cake is put into various things. Most notably, *ozōni*, the New Year's soup—of which there are over one hundred distinct varieties. The fresh rice cake is either put into the soup as is or is first toasted. It turns slippery and succulent and is eaten along with the other ingredients of this festive soup.

Despite all of its felicitous associations, however, *mochi* can be lethal. This is not because of its ingredients but because of its consistency. *Mochi*, particularly in *ozōni*, is a delicious lump of nutrient, which, like peanut butter, refuses to break down in the mouth. Chew as one may, it remains much in its original shape. The temptation is then to swallow it whole. This attempted, it sometimes sticks in the throat. This occurs to any number of throats over the Japanese New Year's season. Newspapers in the days after this nationwide seasonal celebration contain lists of the names of those (mainly oldsters) carried off by this felicitous food.

There is also another variety of foods called *mochi* though these are made of rice flour rather than of pounded rice. Two popular sweets, *daifuku mochi* and *ankoro mochi*, both stuffed with red bean paste, are made with *mochi* proper, but *kusa mochi* is made of nonglutinous rice flour (*jōshinko*) as is the pretty *kashiwa mochi* which is wrapped in an oak leaf and

Making *mochi*. From *Kinsei shokunin zukushi ekotoba* (1805).

served on Boys' Day. *Sakura mochi*, however, which comes wrapped in a *sakura* (cherry tree) leaf, is made of dried and granulated glutinous rice flour (*dōmyō-ji-ko*). In addition some *mochi* foods use ordinary wheat flour as well. The variants (and confusions) go on and on.

It may, however, be bought all year round. The food sections of all department stores and most supermarkets carry *mochi* packaged in vacuum-sealed plastic to put into hot soups. Though *mochi* hardens with age, it softens again when toasted or parboiled. And nowadays, plastic wrapped, it remains soft for a very long time.

Since *mochi* is not, strictly speaking, a cuisine, there are no all-*mochi* restaurants as there are, for example, all-tofu restaurants. It is served in restaurants during the New Year's season and can be had all year round in such concoctions as *shiruko*. Usually, however, it is served mainly in the home. Wherever you have your *mochi*, do remember to chew well and swallow slowly or else all the good fortune attendant upon *mochi* eating will terminate—along with the eater.

TSUKEMONO

The Japanese repast concludes with pickles—*tsukemono*. Though there may be fruit and even nowadays (Western innovation) some kind of dessert, it is with *tsukemono* that the meal ends. As the British want their bit of savory after the sweet, so the Japanese need their pickles after the rice.

So invariable is their appearance that even after a full meal the Japanese find something missing until the *tsukemono* are consumed. Anthropologist Naomichi Ishige, in writing of this bond between pickles and satisfaction, has quoted the French proverb "A meal without cheese is like a one-eyed beauty." A meal without *tsukemono* is felt just this wanting.

The importance of pickles to the Japanese cuisine is also indicated in that *tsukemono* are thought of as *ofukuro no aji* food, something like Mom's real home cooking. After the war many Japanese mothers took to making their own pickles and a whole generation grew up associating *tsukemono* and maternal care. The bond continues even now when the vast majority of pickles are store bought. *Tsukemono* are, in the parlance of California, a "caring" food.

The long association of pickles with rice began very early, perhaps because this grain alone does not give necessary nutrients. Since most of the arable land was given over to rice cultivation, vegetables were not grown in large amounts. Also, during the winter, after the rice harvest, vegetables could not be grown at all. Thus, preserving what few vegetables one had and nibbling them throughout the long winter became a way of staying healthy.

Even now, in the country, a meal of rice and *tsukemono* is not uncommon. These are thought complementary, and it is, consequently, difficult to think

The entrance of an old *tsukemono* shop in Kyoto. Barrels of pickles weighted with stones can be seen outside the shop.

Daikon radishes are hung to dry in the sun for over two weeks before being pickled.

of one without the other. Another reason for the popularity, however, might be that there are so many varieties of *tsukemono* to choose among.

The method of making Japanese pickles determines the taste just as much as do the materials used—for, unlike Western pickles, *tsukemono* use many more vegetables than cucumbers, though they use these too.

The simplest *tsukemono* recipe calls for vegetables (*daikon* radish, gourd, cucumbers, etc.) to be put into a barrel and covered with salt. Once the barrel is full, a lid is put on top, and on top of that a heavy weight, usually a large stone. The weight and the salt combine to force the water out from the vegetables. They are pickled, as it were, in their own juices. This method is called *shio-zuke* because it uses *shio* (salt).

Other methods are: *nuka-zuke*, which uses rice bran; *miso-zuke*, which uses *miso* (fermented bean paste); *kasu-zuke*, which uses saké lees, etc. These in combination with certain vegetables create typical regional variants. Nara's famous *nara-zuke* consists of gourd, *daikon* radish, or cucumber pickled in saké. Shizuoka's *wasabi-zuke* is *wasabi* (horseradish) pickled in saké. Kyoto's *senmai-zuke* is *daikon* radish sliced paper thin, sprinkled with red pepper, and preserved in kelp.

It is said that in Japan there are four thousand different kinds of *tsukemono* and over one hundred different techniques for making them. It is not said who did the counting, but there do appear to be endless local variations.

In the cities, however, one tends to eat the same dozen or so. Just which these were was recently determined by a body with the very Japanese name of Japan Group Feeling Association. It took it upon itself to discover the most popular—and here they are, in order of popularity.

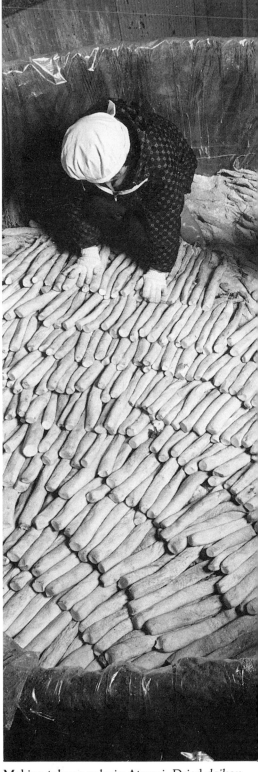

Making *takuan-zuke* in Atsumi. Dried *daikon* radishes are pickled in rice lees.

Wooden barrels full of *tsukemono*.

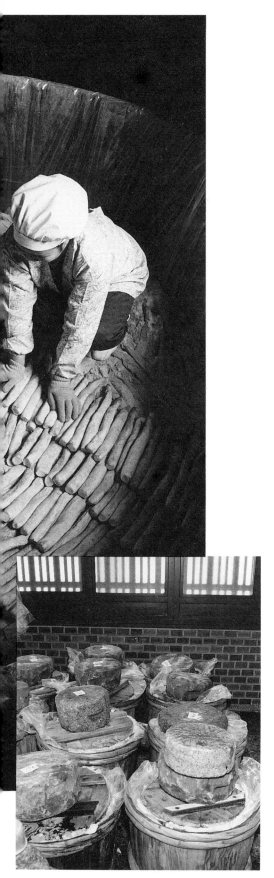

Takuan-zuke (daikon radish), hakusai-zuke (Chinese cabbage), fukujin-zuke (assorted vegetables including eggplant and turnip), shōga-zuke (ginger), kyūri-zuke (cucumber), rakkyo (scallion), umeboshi (plum), nasu-zuke (eggplant), miso-zuke, and nara-zuke.

Many of the *tsukemono* have venerable histories. The most popular, the crisp, tart and highly aromatic *takuan*—pickled *daikon* radish, deep yellow in color—was said to have been created by a Zen priest, one Takuan Oshō, who served during the early seventeenth century at Tōkaiji in present-day Tokyo. It is also said, however, that perhaps the name came from "takuwae-zuke" which means "preserve." It is also said that a nameless priest invented the pickle and then took this name. Whatever, his grave is in the temple ground, and *takuan* lovers still go to pray. The marker is a large stone, and this, say the faithful, is the very stone that weighted down the lid of the barrel where the delicacy was created.

Some of the *tsukemono* varieties have longer histories. *Umeboshi*, preserved plum (though the Japanese plum is much nearer the Western apricot), is first mentioned in tenth-century documents. It seems that it was first a kind of disinfectant, then a kind of medicine before becoming the popular "pickle" that it is.

One of the qualities of *umeboshi* is that it is so salty-sour that one must, it is said, eat large quantities of rice to get rid of the taste. It is thus a good appetite-maker. It is a good appetite-starter as well, which must account for its breakfast-time popularity. Even if you do not feel like eating, one *umeboshi* will convince you otherwise.

This method of weighting the pickles has been used in Kyoto for over 300 years in making *tsukemono* from *sugukina*, a radish-like vegetable.

ABOVE: Three kinds of pickled greens. (Upper left): *hiroshimana*. (Upper right): *takana* from Kita Kyushu. (Bottom): *nozawana* from Shinshu.

The variations on *tsukemono* are endless. Usually small amounts of two or three kinds are served in a small dish.

BELOW: Pickled Chinese cabbage.

The old recipe for *umeboshi* (there are many modern variants) indicates the ease with which *tsukemono* are made. First, the plums must be harvested in June, just before they are ripe. Picked, they are washed, sprinkled with salt, and placed in a crock, which is then covered with a weighted lid. During the following month, the liquid is slowly forced out. This is very sour, and a part of it is later collected and used as a condiment.

Then, during the hot summer months, July or August, the plums are removed from their crock and dried in the sun. At the same time, red *shiso* leaves are salted and added to the liquid. The plums are returned to the now dark-red liquid and this colors them. They will be ready to eat when it gets cold and (traditionally) fresh vegetables become scarce.

Many other things are pickled as a way of preserving them. Fish and meat are kept in *miso* or *saké*—even cherry blossoms are pickled—*sakura no hanazuke*—and served in hot water to mark such social occasions as *omiai*, arranged-marriage meetings, and weddings themselves.

One of the drawbacks of continual *tsukemono* consumption, however, is that the eater eventually consumes too much salt. This is not much of a problem in the cities but in the northern part of Honshu, the snow country, it can be. There the incidence of salt-induced high blood pressure is notably higher than elsewhere.

One of the reasons is that, since fresh vegetables cannot be harvested for a long period of time, much more salt is used. Another is that *tsukemono* are so a part of people's lives there that pickles are eaten even between meals at teatime. Thus, though such northern *tsukemono* are always thoroughly washed before being served, the salt content remains high. Ordinarily, however, there is no difficulty. Store-bought *tsukemono* have a controlled salt level, as do most of the homemade varieties.

The appeal of *tsukemono* is that they taste so fresh. They may have been put up the year before, but the taste is that of living vegetables. One is not eating mummified food, but rather, something close to the vegetable itself, as it was last summer.

Tsukemono are crisp. The sound of biting into and then chewing up, say, the crunchy *takuan*, is quite audible. It is said that thus pickles are Japan's second noisiest dish—the first being *soba*.

It is this crispness, this freshness, which must account for at least some of the popularity of *tsukemono*. Even in the dead of winter, one bite and you are in full summer again.

Making *tsukemono*, an illustration for a *tsukemono* cookbook called *Shiki tsukemono shio kagen*, published in 1836.

Umeboshi.

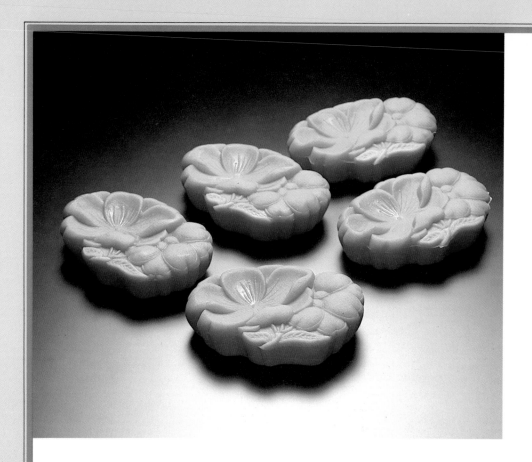

ABOVE: *Taorizakura* or "hand-cut cherry blossoms," a spring sweet containing *an* and wheat flour.
RIGHT: *Wakabakage* or "in the shade of leafy trees," a summer *okashi* made of agar-agar and sugar.

LEFT: *Kozue no aki* or "autumn comes to the treetops." In this autumn sweet made of *an* and flour you can see the maple leaves as they turn from green to gold and from gold to red.

BELOW: *Gionbō*. This winter sweet made of a type of *mochi*, *an*, and sugar is named after a kind of dried persimmon that it is made to resemble, even down to the powdery surface of the dried fruit.

OKASHI

One hears that the Japanese have no sweets, just as one hears that they have no sense of humor. They have both; it is just that neither is to everyone's taste.

If by sweets, however, we mean desserts, then there are none, because the invariable dessert is fruit. The place for Japanese sweets is with a cup of tea between meals or even just before one.

In fact, another name for Japanese confectionery is *chagashi*, or tea sweets. These are sometimes served with ordinary *sencha* leaf teas; they are invariably served with the strong, powdered *matcha* of the tea ceremony.

Perhaps confectionery is the wrong word for Japanese sweets. They contain no butter, baking powder, or yeast, though a few contain wheat flour. Neither are they baked. Rather they are steamed or uncooked. The West has, indeed, nothing quite like them. Like European pastry, however, they have a long history.

The name, *kashi* (the *o* is an honorific prefix), indicates that the sweets were originally fruit. The word derives from *kajitsu*, an early word, and the first man-made sweets from the mainland were called "Chinese fruit." These appeared around the eighth century. It was only later, during the tenth century, that Japanese sweets, or *wagashi*, appeared.

These originally contained no sugar. Indeed, sugar was not generally used in Japan until after the middle of the nineteenth century, though it was known much earlier. The first sugar was apparently brought from China by the celebrated priest, Ganjin. It was presented to the emperor during the celebrations attending the dedication of the Great Buddha at Nara in 752. This, the coarse brown sugar of the period, was regarded as a delicious medicine. For generations

Many of the *okashi* shown in this Edo period catalog are still made today.

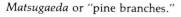

Matsugaeda or "pine branches."

Gionbō.

thereafter the imperial family used what sugar there was as a tasty cure-all. Sugar cane was grown in Japan (Amami-Oshima, later Shikoku) from the late sixteenth century but the produce never then reached plebeian tables.

The main ingredient of Japanese sweets, *wagashi*, is *an*. This is a paste made from sugar and various materials: red *azuki* beans, white beans, sweet potatoes, chestnuts, snow peas, etc. There are three types. The smooth purée is called *koshi-an*, the chunky peanut-butter type is *tsubushi-an*, and the powdered "instant" variety is *sarashi-an*.

Japanese confections come in four categories. The *namagashi* (or "raw") do not keep well, hence probably the name. Included are jellies and the more delicate pastes and rice-flour-based doughs. *Han-namagashi* ("semi-raw") keep better and include *yōkan* jellies and *manjū*, steamed buns filled with *an* (red bean paste). *Higashi* ("dry") includes what we would call candies and items we would not consider sweets at all, such as *senbei* (rice crackers). The last category, *namban-gashi* ("southern barbarian sweets," a name referring to the early Portuguese visitors) contains Western-influenced desserts such as jelly rolls filled with *an* instead of jelly or jam.

From *an* and rice flour or *mochi* (rice cake) hundreds (one old cookbook gives a thousand) of sweets are made, each different in shape, color, and—it is said—taste.

To make *kikugasane*, powdered glutinous rice is mixed with water. The dough is steamed and rolled out. Here pink *mochi* is being layered on white *mochi*. Extra flour used to keep the layers from sticking to each other is being brushed away. The sweet is carefully formed. This important step requires a skilled hand. The addition of a chrysanthemum (*kiku*) crest makes this an autumn *okashi*, but this sweet is sold all year round with different names and different crests.

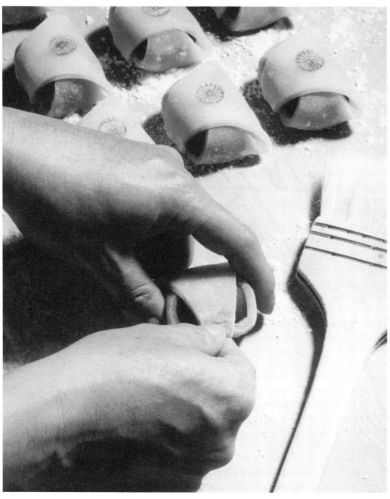

RIGHT: (from top to bottom): *Hanagoromo*. The cherry blossom (*hana*) crest makes this a spring sweet. *Kokeshimizu*, summer. *Kikugoromo*, autumn. *Yukimochi*, winter.

The beans are boiled, mashed, and made into a purée, as chestnuts are for *marrons chantilly*, to create *an*. Or the purée is combined with Japanese *kanten* (agar-agar) to produce *yōkan* (jelly). The rice flour or *mochi* is molded into a dough to be used for covering or for decoration.

Each of the varieties also has a distinctive and often poetic name. Since the sweets are perishable and since the Japanese like to make much of seasonal fare, all *okashi* come with seasonal attributes.

During the spring one might consume *hanagoromo*, the name referring to the kimono one wears to go cherry-blossom viewing. It consists of *an* wrapped in thin pink and white *mochi*, the whole stamped with a cherry-blossom crest. For summer, one would nibble at *kokeshimizu*, the name of which means "moss in a stream." This pale green and cooling *okashi* is made from *kanten* and *dōmyōji-ko*, dried and granulated glutinous rice flour. The transparent jelly seems to contain mossy delicacies in its depths. For autumn a fitting *okashi* is *kikugoromo*, the name referring to an annual custom concerning the *kiku* (chrysanthemum). A bit of cotton which had been placed on this autumn flower was taken, now impregnated with the smell, and rubbed on the body, the belief being that this would increase longevity. This sweet is thus made in the shape of a chrysanthemum, pink *an* made from eggs forming the flower and white *an* made from the Chinese yam representing the cotton. For winter, a typical sweet would be *yukimochi* (winter rice cake), a *mochi* ball covered with *kōrimochi*, rice cake which has been frozen and crushed.

There are also year-round favorites such as one called "the beautiful bay of Tango," a confection first made in 1695, a pink and yellow affair resembling a chestnut burr and named for a scenic spot immortalized in a poem from the eighth-century collection, the *Manyoshū*.

Another reason so much is made of the seasonal attributes of *okashi* is that they are a traditional part of the tea ceremony which is also, in its way, a celebration of the seasons, its ideal being an openness to nature. The traditional duty of the tea ceremony *okashi* is to indicate the lively participation of all five senses: its shape and color appeal to the eye, the poetic name appeals to the ear, the faint and delicate smell to the nose, texture to the sense of touch, and a presumed deliciousness to the mouth. To this end, fancy reigns. Cakes are named after poems in the imperial collections, or after historical incidents, or well-known legends as well.

There is also an amount of preciousness involved in both the construction (the best red *azuki* beans only from Hokkaido and the best white-bean paste only from Gumma) and the consumption of Japanese *okashi*. But this is true of all desserts the world over as a glance at a continental cookbook (Gateau à la Gloire du Roi) will attest.

There is also a certain amount of contention, even within Japan, as to just how good these confections taste. Some, many foreigners among them, maintain that they are delicious. Others judiciously say that if most Japanese food is for the eye then the appeal of *okashi* is entirely ocular. Still others, less charitable, state that they taste like so many varieties of wallpaper paste. The eater must decide.

One of the most pleasant ways to consume *okashi* is to take some of these seasonal dainties and pay a call, nibbling at them over a cup of tea with one's host. Another way is to buy some, take them home, and gorge. Certainly *okashi* are purchasable everywhere—including a number of name-brand shops.

Another way is to drop into a "teahouse" and order what one wants, to be served along with one's tea. These teahouses (shops, actually) stock wide varieties of *wagashi* and display many in the windows—which is how you recognize the shop. In Tokyo, Ginza seems a favorite place for such refreshments and here one may see a variety of elegant matrons, pretty young girls, and nary a man, enjoying what is said to be one of the delights of Japanese cuisine.

The Toraya teahouse in Akasaka. This well-known shop has branches in Ginza and Paris.

SAKÉ

Umemiya Shrine in Kyoto. This shrine is dedicated to the god of saké making.

Saké, to Japan as wine is to France, has a long history. Legend holds that the ancient gods themselves imbibed, making their brew from the first rice of the new year. And even now saké retains its sacerdotal character. Marriage ceremonies include ritual saké drinking; saké is placed on the family altar for the delectation of both the gods and the dead; many of the annual festivals include heavy imbibing because the gods like to drink and because the drunk are plainly in closer communication with the beyond than are the sober.

The first literary reference to saké drinking occurs early, in the *Kojiki*, Japan's first chronology, said completed in 712. That saké, however, was not the colorless fragrant beverage we know today. It was more like the milky, unrefined liquor still available (under the counter) as *doburoku* or (over it) as *nigori-zake*.

Likewise late is the custom of drinking refined saké warm. Originally, this was customary only during the cold winter months—from the ninth day of the ninth month through the second day of the third month, says one old account. From the middle of the eighteenth century, however, drinking saké heated became first a fashion, then a custom. One reason was that cold saké contained harmful impurities, it was said, and that warming it somehow took them out. Another reason sometimes given is that warm saké prevents the bad breath which saké drinking does, as a matter of fact, give. Yet another might have been that drinking saké hot is more economical. Hot, it makes you drunker faster; less saké goes a longer way. On the other hand, it is also said warm saké is so smooth it encourages overdrinking, and that slightly astringent cold saké makes you drink more

ABOVE: Many types of saké are kept and served at an *izakaya*.

RIGHT: Scene from an Edo-period brewery showing saké making in the Aizu area (Fukushima Prefecture).

Saké labels.

Senjutosazuru.

Tōyōjō.

Keigetsu.

Matsuokina.

Kikusui.

slowly. In any event the proper temperature for warmed saké (*kan*) is 104°–131°F (40°–50°C).

The alcoholic content is low, compared to spirits, yet saké still has the highest among nondistilled liquors. The Japanese government specifies the range of 15 to 16.5 percent, a figure which might be compared to the 4 percent of Japanese beer or the 10 percent of most wines. Thus, a saké high is fairly easy to arrange and the consequent saké hangover is rather difficult to avoid.

Saké is, of course, made from rice, but its method of brewing is different from that used in making such other grain-based beverages as, say, beer. The distinctive difference about saké brewing is that the turning of rice starch to a sugar occurs simultaneously with the fermenting of the sugar to produce alcohol in the final mash. There are many complicated steps among the various stages of saké production and since each of the 2,700 brewers in Japan adds its own distinctive refinements, the resulting sakés offer a multitude of tastes.

One of the joys of saké drinking, and one of the duties of the saké *tsū* (connoisseur), is discovering which among the many are truly the best and/or which most perfectly suit the individual palate.

There are three considerations which are considered basic. These are: which type of saké, what grade of saké, and whether to have it sweet or dry. All of this information is plainly printed on the saké bottle label, though it is, of course, in Japanese.

There are many types of saké, of which only a number of the most important will be considered here. First is *junmai-shu*, a pure rice saké with no ad-

Toyonoume.

Suigei.

Gyokuhai.

Hibikinada.

Tsukasabotan.

Bunkajin.

Hamanotsuru.

Ashizuri.

ditions. This is the saké one sees abroad, particularly in America which allows importation only of *jun-mai-shu*. The taste is said to be closest to that of the sakés of the Edo period.

Next is *honjō-zukuri* (also called *honjō-zō, hon-shikomi* and *hon-zukuri*). Alcohol is added (still about 15 percent but now one quarter of this is added alcohol) in an attempt to preserve the rich *junmai-shu* taste while at the same time achieving a mildness said to be favored by contemporary Japanese saké drinkers.

Following this comes *ginjō-zukuri* (or *ginjō-zō*), a special type of *junmai-shu* or *honjō-zukuri* and the one which many *tsū* regard as the ultimate saké. This type is brewed only in small quantities and may be difficult to find and, if found, expensive.

The next type, *genshu*, has a slightly higher alcohol level (about 20 percent), has a full-bodied taste, and is not so often drunk warm. Indeed, it is one of the favorites used in that summer drink: *sake on za rokku* or saké-on-the-rocks. *Namazake*, a variety of *genshu*, is especially good. Here the yeast is still active (it is unpasteurized) and this gives a tart flavor. It must, of course, be drunk immediately upon the opening of the bottle.

Finally (though there are more saké types than these here mentioned) there is *taru-zake*, or saké from the cask. It is aged in wood and thus absorbs a taste somewhat reminiscent of (though not so raw as) the Greek retsina. Again (as with all sakés) it should be drunk soon after the cask (nowadays the bottle as well) is opened.

All of these types (and many more) are graded and

this brings us to our next consideration on the evaluation of saké. The government agency administering this system of grading is the same as that collecting taxes on saké. It says that saké is to be classified into three ranks: *tokkyū* (special class), *ikkyū* (first class), and *nikyū* (second class). These do indeed indicate the relative qualities of the sakés which are produced by a single maker but saké making is complicated, as we have seen, and each brand is special. Of a consequence, the system can be misleading when sakés of different makes are compared, particularly those of the second class.

One of the reasons is that, since the tax on first class saké is double that of second class, some makers do not submit their sakés for testing. In that case they are automatically graded by the government as second class. Thus, some sakés from some brewers are really first class in quality though labeled second class on their label. It is the business of the saké *tsū* to know just which makers these are. At second class prices he may then produce a first class or even a special class saké.

The final consideration is whether you want your saké sweet (*amakuchi*) or dry (*karakuchi*). This will naturally influence which saké you buy or order at a bar or *nomiya*. The *tsū* prefers a saké which is very dry and very heavy. But non-*tsū*, average drinkers, like a sweetish taste which is considered "lighter," and thus reflects a change in Japanese taste which favors light drinks in general—light, pale beers and lighter soft drinks as well.

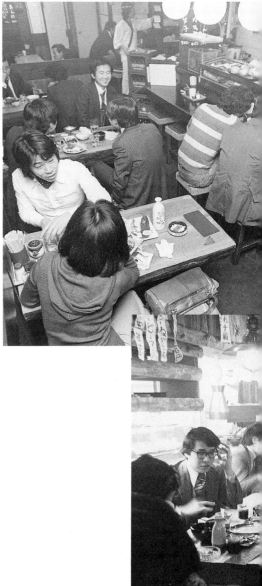

If you have the proper type of saké in the proper grade, if it is the proper degree of dryness (or sweetness) then you will naturally also know how to observe the proper etiquette in saké drinking.

This is also a bit complicated but, at least, it is invariable. First, one must remember that saké is made from rice. Therefore, drinking saké while eating rice is redundant. Saké drinking stops before the rice appears at the end of the meal.

It is thus apparent that saké, like wine, ought be accompanied by food. Though there are social saké drinkers, the *tsū* demands that there also be something to eat or at least nibble on. And whether the edibles are *otsumami* (snacks) or something in many courses, he also demands that one knows what food goes with saké and which does not.

Saké is good with fish in any form. In fact, the generic term for saké food is *sakana*, i.e., "fish." Among preferred foods are cod and salmon roe, dried fish, *sashimi*, and the rarer regional foods from around Japan. Saké also welcomes the various stews,

Edo-period *izakaya* as shown in *Kinsei shokunin zukushi ekotoba* (1805).

The inside of a typical *izakaya*. A relaxed, informal atmosphere is the rule in these places. Note that the waiter and master wear Japanese clothing.

This *izakaya*, Kita no Kazoku, has many branches and is quite popular. The *sakana* are written on strips posted up on the wall.

or *nabemono*, of winter though some *tsū* maintain that saké and that popular winter stew, sukiyaki, do not properly mix.

The other thing for the beginner to remember is that he must always lift his saké cup (*sakazuki* or *choko*) when he is being served from the *tokkuri* bottle on the table—each containing one *go*, or a little over six ounces of saké. Also, unless dining with close acquaintances, he never fills his own cup. These prohibitions are of ancient lineage. Ideally, the attendant pours. If there is no such, then the "lower" pours initially for the "higher." This so complicated that I will not go into it at all except to say that the host is always initially "lower" though he may be socially "higher" and thus pours for a possibly "lower" guest who is temporarily "higher." In the event that you have been poured for, "low" though you may be, you must always pour in return. If, on the other hand, you wish to drink at your own rate and pour for yourself, a perfectly proper alternative, is to say "*tejaku shimasu*" and proceed to do so.

One of the early methods of saké drinking was to employ a single large cup (as in certain forms of the tea ceremony) which was passed in turn to everyone. Vestiges of this custom persist in the habit of passing the *choko* back and forth.

You empty yours, dip it in the saké-cup washing bowl, if there is one, then pass it to the person you wish to honor. It is held up and you fill it. He, or more often she, empties it, washes it, hands it back, you hold it up, and it is refilled. Then you drink. This can go on forever and always results in a terrific hangover since saké is to the Japanese hangover as champagne is to that of the West.

Like champagne, saké also remains a celebratory drink. With beer or whiskey or the distilled *shōchū*, all drinks more popular than saké, a simple clinking of glasses suffices—or nothing at all. Saké, however, demands more etiquette and more fellow feeling. It is the ideal bond among fellow workers drinking after the day's labors, or among women friends who meet to talk and enjoy each others' company. Saké remains special.

"*Kampai*," you say politely, making the toast that the celebration of saké drinking demands, then sip and savor the first taste of fine saké, one of the best drinks you'll ever have.

Saké is sometimes served in a wooden cup called a *masu*. The salt on the corner of the cup improves the slightly sweet taste of saké.

Tarō Yamamoto, a well-known poet, drinking saké.

OCHA

After the meal is done, after everything is finished, comes the national beverage— *ocha* (green tea).

Though green tea is long associated with Japan, it is prepared from the leaves of the same plant that produces the black teas of China, India, and Sri Lanka. The difference is that in Japan the tea leaves are steamed after picking. This destroys an enzyme present in the tea plant, and the leaf consequently stays green. It thus retains its natural vitamins and the potassium and phosphoric acid that it also contains. In India and elsewhere the leaves are not steamed. They consequently turn dark and make the more familiar black tea.

The drink itself came to Japan from China in the ninth century, brought by returning monks, probably in the form of tea seed since there is record of this first being planted by a Kyoto monk. The Japanese word for tea also comes from China. *Ocha* is the Chinese *cha* with an honorific *o* added. Our English word is equally Chinese—*te*, a southern Chinese dialect term, pronounced "tay."

It was not, however, until the twelfth century, when powdered tea was brought back by Japanese monks returning from China, that tea drinking became common. Though its medicinal properties were stressed, it also came to be regarded as pleasantly invigorating.

But only among the higher social classes, those who could afford the still rare beverage. Sociable tea drinking became increasingly formalized and one of the results was the Japanese tea ceremony, a social and psychological event in which tea making and tea drinking become a contemplative experience.

Tea remained associated with the priesthood. It

Rubbing the leaves between the hands makes the tea more fragrant.

The tea-making process as described in the nineteenth-century volume *Oshiegusa*. (From right to left, top to bottom): the tea is picked, steamed, cooled, roasted, rubbed between the hands, carefully chosen, packed, and comes to a fitting end in the tea ceremony.

was, in fact, monk Eisai who was responsible for the fad of aristocratic tea drinking. His small book on tea, one which the upper class read, remains the earliest appreciation of tea. In particular, tea was associated with the Zen sect of Buddhism, and from this rose the tea-associated arts—including *sumi-e* (black ink painting) and *ikebana* (flower arranging). Earlier, tea had been used by priests to keep awake during all night vigils. (According to one illustrative legend, the priest Daruma, unable to stay awake, tore off his offending eyelids. Cast aside, they took root and became the tea plant, the leaves of which even now retain the shape of the abandoned eyelids.) In the popular mind tea became associated with the "awakening" called *satori*, though no actual connection is possible, and this became yet another reason for thinking well of *matcha*, the strong powdered tea, which at this time was the only form of tea Japan's ecclesiastics and aristocracy knew.

Tea drinking in Japan did not become popular with ordinary people until the leaves themselves began to be used. Just when this happened is unknown. Though the history of *matcha* in Japan, being part of the history of the aristocracy, is well documented, the humble history of leaf tea drinking is not.

One of the few facts recorded is that in the eighteenth century a Zen monk named or nicknamed Baisao (an appellation which might be translated as "old tea seller") began steeping and selling tea as one of his ecclesiastic activities. It was said that he learned how to do this during a stay in Nagasaki, then the only port open to the world. And this might mean that it was learned from China and that ordinary tea drinking as we now know it did not enter Japan until very late, the middle Edo period.

Hills covered with tea bushes are a common sight in Shizuoka.

TOP LEFT: *Sencha* from Shizuoka. TOP RIGHT: *Gyokuro*. CENTER LEFT: *Bancha*. CENTER RIGHT: *Genmai-cha*. BOTTOM LEFT: *Mugi-cha*.

Even if ordinary tea drinking started late, it rapidly became a national custom. By the end of the eighteenth century, tea was commonly drunk everywhere—townspeople and commoner as well as clergy and warrior were drinking steeped tea. And as the tea habit flourished, so did the tea plantations. Japan now produces over one hundred thousand tons of tea a year.

Half of this is from Shizuoka Prefecture, the locality most famed for its plantations. But there are other tea-growing areas in other places, from the environs of Tokyo down to the southern island of Kyushu.

Some varieties are thought better than others. In Shizuoka, *Kawane-cha* is considered best. Near Tokyo it is *Sayama-cha*. The *absolute* best, however, is said to come from near Kyoto, the historic town of Uji, in fact—hence *Uji-cha*.

All Japanese tea is graded. At the bottom, but nonetheless quite good, is *bancha*—common, coarse tea. This is the kind given you at the store or at the ordinary Japanese restaurant while you are reading the menu. Yellow rather than green and usually slightly astringent, it is also always free—considered so common that no one would ever ask money for a cup.

Bancha also has two variations. Roasted it makes the smoky tasting, dark brown *hōji-cha*. This can be drunk cold which ordinary *bancha* cannot be since it turns bitter. The other *bancha* variation is *genmai-cha*, a very coarse variety which includes stems and is mixed with grains of roasted rice which give it a nutty, rustic flavor.

Going up the scale, the next better grade is *sencha*. It is made to be savored and is not considered the thirst quencher that *bancha* is. The leaves are of a

LEFT: Kiyomizu teapot and cups for *gyokuro*. The other vessel is used to cool boiling water to the proper temperature. ABOVE: Seto ware tea cups and Tokoname teapot for *sencha*.

Teatime on the veranda. *Tsukemono* and *onigiri* go well with tea.

better variety, have been picked with greater care, and there are no stems. Good restaurants, such as sushi shops, will serve *sencha* free, but at other places one pays for it as one would for black tea (*kō-cha*) or coffee. *Sencha* is what you are served when you make a social call and are properly received. It is also Japan's most popular tea. Eighty percent of all tea leaves grown in the country end up as *sencha*.

Continuing upward, one reaches the finest of the Japanese green teas—*gyokuro*. Here only the best and most tender bud leaves from the finest and oldest bushes are used. Further, the tea plant has been shaded and shielded from direct sunlight. Finally, the picking has been done with the greatest care, much being made of the precise timing—just when the leaf was fully "ripe."

The crop is consequently small and *gyokuro* is quite expensive. Infused, the tea is a celadon green and quite aromatic. It must be sipped slowly, appreciated, perhaps exclaimed over. *Gyokuro* means "dewdrop" and this tea is thought just this precious.

There are several other *cha*-type drinks, but these are not made of tea. The popular *mugi-cha* is an infusion made of roast barley. It is good hot or cold and is a fine thirst quencher. Its only drawback is that it is also a mild laxative. *Kobu-cha* is an infusion made from kelp which is surprisingly good. An acquired taste, perhaps; it quickly becomes an addiction. There are in addition many other beverages made from other kinds of tea and other non-tea materials—so many that a mere listing would fill the page.

Japanese green tea is made like tea everywhere else with several important differences. First, boiling water is never used. Indeed if the water is too hot (let alone boiling) it kills the flavor. Ideally the water should be about 175°F (80°C). Second, Japanese tea is steeped for a shorter time—one minute is the maximum. Also, the proportions of tea to water are slightly different. For two teaspoons of *sencha* leaves, one full cup of water—which makes two small cups of tea.

The major difference is in the drinking. One never takes milk or lemon or sugar. One drinks Japanese green tea as it is, though often Japanese sweets, *okashi*, are nibbled along with it. These are made specifically to be consumed with green tea—they become unthinkable with coffee.

The last cup of tea is drunk, the end of the meal is reached. The taste of Japan, fresh, natural, slightly astringent, still lingers.

INDEX

ACKNOWLEDGMENTS

The Publisher herein wishes to express its gratitude to the many organizations, institutions, and individuals that assisted with this book, and wishes to give special thanks to Kozōzushi Center Co., Ltd., which sells the sushi on pages 18–19 and allowed one of its shops to be photographed; Michiko Odagiri, who prepared the sushi on page 17; the staff of PEC, who helped the editors gather good photographs; Restaurant Suehiro, which prepared the sukiyaki on pages 20, 22–23; Tokiko Suzuki, who prepared the tempura on pages 30–31 (bottom), 33; and Uoju, which prepared the *maku-no-uchi bentō* on page 73.

Among the photographers, companies, and photo agencies who provided photographs for this book are Mitsuo Adachi, pages 92–93; Asahi Shimbun Photo Service, page 47 (below); Bon Color Photo Agency, pages 57, 65, 68–69, 76–77, 102; Hiroshi Dobuchi, pages 50–53, 67 (right); Fine Photo Agency, page 106; Jirō Futamura, page 103; Genroku Co., Ltd., pages 18–19 (bottom); Hokka-hokka-tei, page 75 (top right); Kōji Izumi, pages 30–31 (top left to right), 32; Keizō Kaneko, pages 18–19 (top), 20, 22–23; Keiichi Kimura, page 94; Kodansha Library, pages 24–25 (below), 25 (top), 34–35, 38–39 (*yudōfu* course), 48, 64, 78–79, 83, 85, 98–99, 100–101 (center and bottom); Kodansha staff photographers, pages 36, 38–39 (kinds of tofu), 60 (top), 86 (left), 87 (right); Tōru Kurobe, pages 13–15; Kyoto Film Agency, page 95 (top); Aritoshi Nakazato, page 17; Nihon Menruigyō Kumiai Rengōkai, page 56; Yoshikatsu Saeki, page 16 (bottom); Sekai Bunka Photo, page 80 (bottom); Makoto Shimomura, pages 86–87 (varieties of *tsukemono*); Hiroshi Suga, page 42; Satoru Tabuchi, pages 84–85, 89; Tea Association of Japan, pages 104–05 (bottom); Akihiko Tokue, pages 72–73; Tokyo Photo Agency, page 29; Tokyo Tansuigyo Niuke Kumiai Rengōkai, pages 66–67 (*unagi* posters); Toraya Confectionary Ltd., pages 90–91, 96; Takayuki Tōyama, pages 107, 108 (bottom); Miyuki Wakatabe, pages 30–31 (bottom), 33; Kumeo Yamada, pages 43–45; Yōichi Yamazaki, pages 108–09 (top); Masayoshi Yano, page 16 (top left, right); Hisamitsu Yasumuro, page 95 (from center top to bottom); Takayuki Yatagai, page 46; Masaharu Yoshimura, pages 54–55, 58–59, 60 (bottom), 61; Yuzu Kōbō, page 97; Zenkoku Mochi Kōgyō Kumiai, pages 80 (top), 81.

The Publisher wishes to thank the following for generously allowing reproduction of objects in their collections: Chōen-ji, pages 70–71; Kazuma Mitani, pages 88–89; National Diet Library, pages 24 (top), 105; Shō Matsui and Nobori-tei, pages 62–63; Tokyo National Museum, pages 26–27, 40–41, 82, 100-01 (top).

Acknowledgment is also made to the following books and publishers that were valuable sources of visual material and information: *Aji no takumi* (Kodansha, 1982), for the photographs on pages 13–15, 36, 38–39 (kinds of tofu), 43–45, 60 (top), 84, 86 (left), 87 (right), 89, 107, 108 (bottom); *Asahi kurashi no fudoki: Kutsurogi no cha* (Asahi Shimbun Publishing Co., 1982), for the photograph on pages 108–09 (top); *Bessatsu taiyo: Wagashi saijiki* (Heibonsha, 1981), for the photographs on pages 94–95; *Cooking Etude: Wafu no katei ryōri* (Kodansha, 1983), for the photographs on pages 30–31 (bottom) and 33; *Edo ryōri dokuhon* (Shibata Publishing Company, 1982), for the illustration on page 88; *Illustrated Encyclopedia View* (Kodansha, 1984), for the *eki-ben* photographs on pages 74–75; *Misesu aizōban: Mainichi no okome ryōri* (Bunka Publishing Bureau, 1982), for the photograph on page 17; *Nihon byōbu-e shūsei*, vol. 14 (Kodansha, 1977), for the *byōbu-e* picture on pages 70–71; *Nihon no ryōri* (Kodansha, 1975), for the photographs on pages 16 (top left, right), 30–31 (top left to right), 32, 50–53, 67 (right), 92–93, 97; *Nihon no soba* (Mainichi Shimbunsha, 1981), for the photographs on pages 54–55, 58–59, 60 (bottom), 61; *Nihonshu* (Mainichi Shimbunsha, 1983), for the photograph on page 103; *Tōfu hyaku chin* (Shibata Publishing Company, 1982), for the illustration on page 37; *Unagi to nobori-tei* (Midori Shōbo Co., Ltd., 1984) for the ukiyo-e on pages 62–63; *Utsukushii washokki no hon* (Kodansha, 1982), for the *tsukemono* photographs spread across pages 86–87; *With* (Kodansha, 1983), for the photograph on page 16 (bottom).